Pheasant Tail
Simplicity

Recipes and Techniques for Successful Fly Fishing

YVON CHOUINARD | CRAIG MATHEWS | MAURO MAZZO

Pheasant Tail Simplicity
Recipes and Techniques for Successful Fly Fishing

Patagonia publishes a select list of titles on wilderness, wildlife, and outdoor sports that inspire and restore a connection to the natural world and encourage action to combat climate chaos.

Paperback Edition

Published by Patagonia Works

Printed in Canada on 100 percent postconsumer recycled paper.

Editorial Advisors: Nicholas Blixt, Kate Hadeka
Editor: John Dutton, Sharon AvRutick
Photo Editor: Rich Crowder
Art Director/Designer: Eric Lovejoy, Stephen Rockwood
Studio Photography: Meghan Mireles, Tim Davis, Bryan Gregson
Illustrations: Samantha Aronson
Assistant Fly Tiers: Sam Brown, Nicholas Blixt
Project Manager: Sonia Moore
Photo Production: Bernardo Salce
Graphic Production: Natausha Greenblott, Michaela Purcilly, Natalie Mitchell
Creative Director: Michael Leon
Publisher: Karla Olson

Paperback ISBN 978-1-952338-28-1

E-Book ISBN 978-1-952338-29-8

Library of Congress Control Number 2025938688

ENVIRONMENTAL BENEFITS STATEMENT

Patagonia Inc saved the following resources by printing the pages of this book on chlorine free paper made with 100% post-consumer waste.

TREES	WATER	ENERGY	SOLID WASTE	GREENHOUSE GASES
235 FULLY GROWN	19,000 GALLONS	99 MILLION BTUs	800 POUNDS	101,400 POUNDS

Environmental impact estimates were made using the Environmental Paper Network Paper Calculator 4.0. For more information visit www.papercalculator.org

1% FOR THE PLANET MEMBER

FSC www.fsc.org MIX Paper | Supporting responsible forestry FSC® C016245

Land Acknowledgment

Building mutual relationships with Indigenous peoples is part of our work to restore Earth, the home we all share. Patagonia's headquarters is located on the unceded homelands of the Chumash people in what is now known as Ventura, California. Because the people in this book are in locations around the planet, we acknowledge the many Indigenous communities who have stewarded the lands and waters of each of these places since time immemorial. We are also grateful for their continued leadership in the environmental and climate movement today.

Cover and opposite page: The singular tail feather of a male ring-necked pheasant.

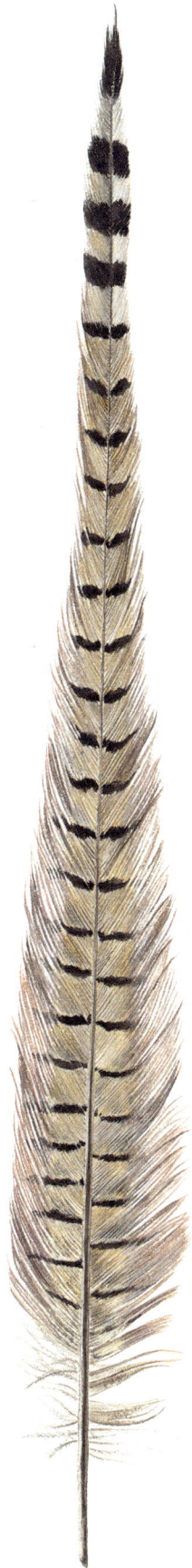

What is the stream telling us to do today? What fly
to use: pheasant tail soft hackle, nymph, or dry fly?
RICH CROWDER

Contents

Rising brown trout and pale morning dun.
Silver Creek, Idaho. NICK PRICE

Introduction

Why bother to write an entire book about the singular barbs of the tail feathers of a male ring-necked pheasant? You may be thinking the old boys have fallen into the behavior of the nerd scientist who devotes his life to learning more and more about less and less. But wait, before you pitch this book back into the fly-fishing shop's dusty remainders bin, let us explain.

Our previous book *Simple Fly Fishing* made the case to replace a lot of the unnecessary gear and impediments endemic in fly fishing with knowledge and technique. Going toward simplicity is not an absolute. Thoreau said, "Simplify, simplify," to which his friend Emerson responded, "You could have said that with one simplify." Since we wrote that book in 2014, we have done just that.

We propose that the barbs of ring-necked pheasant tail feathers can be used to tie the bodies of nymphs, dry flies, emergers, and beetles that are equally as or even more effective than the thousands of flies in the fly shop.

This book is not intended for the beginner fly angler nor for the gear junkie who believes the secret to success lies in buying ever more equipment and flies. It's not even for the serious angler who doesn't tie flies, because you can't buy some of the patterns we're describing. It's for the person who knows that restricting your options forces you to be creative. If you understand that limiting your fly options and relying on skill, knowledge, and technique leads not just to success but to satisfaction, this book is for you.

Before catch and release caught on in the 1960s, a fish was fooled by an artificial fly once or twice at most before ending up in the frying pan. Now with each release they get smarter and are less eager to fall for the same fly again. Perhaps more than intellectually "superior" humans, fish learn from their mistakes. The big, bushy, dependable old flies like the Double Humpy or Royal Coachman—or even Czech nymphs—don't work as they used to. Yet why do the Classic Pheasant Tail Nymph, the Adams, and the Woolly Bugger still fish as well as ever? It may have to do with their simple plainness.

The favorite of many anglers, the Adams has been around since 1922, and a hundred years later it still works great. The flies with modern, distinguishing features like glitter, doll's eyes, or garish colors now often scare fish rather than entice them to eat. A tackle company in the United States estimates that after a fish has been fooled into taking one of its lures, it will not go for that lure again for three weeks. The New Zealand anglers say that gold and silver beads on nymphs are no longer an asset, and they have switched to the more natural black beads. There is also a tendency to fish smaller flies than before.

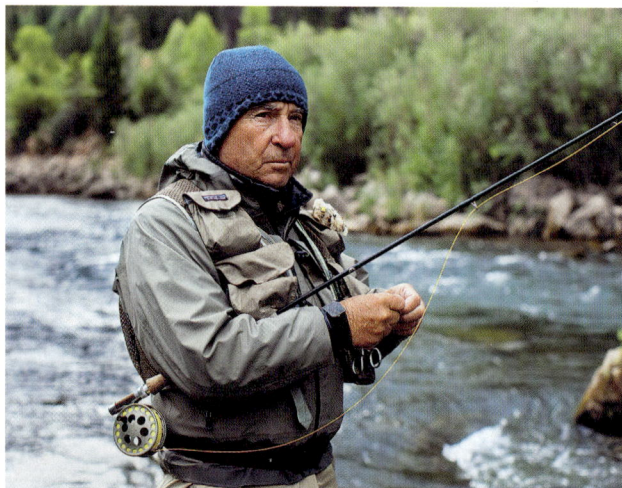

The big gaudy streamers that were all the rage for catching big brown trout just a few years ago still elicit explosive boils, fooling the angler into thinking that she just missed a monster. But more often, it was just an irritated brown trying to chase the fly out of its territory without ever grabbing it. Switch to something small and drab, though, and you better hold on.

Yvon Chouinard checking the late evening rises on the Upper Gros Ventre River. Jackson, Wyoming.
TIM DAVIS

Of all the aspects in an artificial fly that are important to fool fish, we would rank them as follows:

1. The *position* of the fly in relation to where the fish are feeding. "People rob banks because that's where the money is."

2. The *action* of the fly—for example, a dry fly or nymph with no drag, or a hopper or emerger with a small twitch.

3. The *size* of the fly, closely matching the size of the natural, or, when there is no hatch going, larger as an attractor.

4. The *shape* or type of fly to match the intended food.

5. The *color* of the fly—the least important aspect, even though fish do see some colors.

Fish are predators just like your house cat. Drag a toy mouse across the floor and the cat will go into his attack crouch. Stop the toy and then give it a twitch. Bingo! Does the cat care if the toy mouse is yellow or tan? As fly anglers, we are trying to elicit this instinctive predatory response from the fish we target.

Successfully catching fish is less about having a thousand flies in your vest and more about having faith in an all-around fly and fishing it where, when, and how it should be fished. Technique, confidence, and skill trump dozens of fly boxes. In other words, you need to learn to read the water and to match the fly and the technique to each specific situation. Here's a story about how that theory was drilled into us some years ago.

Y.C. hooks into wild vistas and wild trout. Las Pampas, Argentina. BRYAN GREGSON

A STORY

Every Man for …

Chris Sepio, Mauro Mazzo, and I were fishing together along a section of river in Argentinian Patagonia. Rather than "every man for himself," we decided to stick together and fish each area of the river according to *how* it should be fished. Mauro would nymph through the deep pools, Chris would cast dry flies in the slower water and hard-to-reach pockets, and I would swing soft hackles in the fast riffles. We fished each type of water in its most logical way. We made a pact to not let a single fish go uncaught. I'm embarrassed to say how many fish we took that day.

-Y.C.

Kate Hadeka casting a mono rig in the wind, in a very remote Patagonia canyon. MAURO MAZZO

Fishing where the fish are in the stream also means fishing where they are in the water column. If a trout is grubbing around the bottom, knocking caddis larvae off the rocks, it is not going to go for your high-floating Adams on the surface. Also, a trout taking emergers just under the surface couldn't care less about your weighted stonefly tumbling along the streambed.

Another thing to consider is that there are fewer insects and thus fewer hatches than there were just a few decades ago. Scientists tell us we've lost 70 percent of our flying-insect life and 45 percent of invertebrates in the United States. I remember a time when evening drives in summer left the windshield so encrusted with bugs you had to stop to scrape them off. Today, that's a rare event. You can put the blame on night lights, pesticides, loss of habitat, climate change, pollution, exotic species, drought, and the irresponsible management of dams.

Back then, fishing the fabled Railroad Ranch section of the Henry's Fork in Idaho was often a lesson in frustration. There would be three or four different species of flies—caddis, stones, mayflies—all hatching at once. The sky was full of flycatchers, swallows, and seagulls cartwheeling through the air in a feeding frenzy. You could hardly inhale without sucking in one kind of bug or another. Success then meant identifying which stage of which insect that big rainbow was keyed in on.

But those days are gone, for the most part. The hatches that do happen now often come early in April and May, well before the season opens on June 15. Even worse news, the mayflies are now a size smaller than they used to be.

On more typical rivers, especially during the dog days of August, you might get a single hatch for an hour or two. So, what do you do for the rest of the day? It's a good argument to fish a neutral-colored fly like the Classic Pheasant Tail in its various forms and sizes. This fly will work from morning until evening whether there's a hatch or not. Trout still need to eat, but perhaps not the same foods and in the same way as they did forty or sixty years ago.

In this book we feature eighteen flies that have been proven to work well catching trout, salmon, steelhead, and bonefish. We've included tying instructions for each pattern, as well as QR codes that you can use to access online content that contains more tying instructions and short videos of a few techniques for fishing these flies.

Hatch on the Henry's Fork, Idaho. JEREMIAH WATT

Fish as if the Fish Are Spooked

By October in Wyoming, the local public spring creek had gotten so difficult that for the last three times I fished it, I caught zilch. The fish were there, you could see them, and they didn't seem overly spooked. Not like the fish in a wild mountain stream that freak out when they see you approach from a hundred feet away. I saw these eighteen-inch cutthroats chasing each other around and occasionally I could see a white mouth open to take in some size 32 unidentifiable belly lint of an organism.

No matter what micro-fly was on my 7X tippet, they refused. Not even a look, a bump, or a turn away. There was just no interest. Thankfully, I never saw anyone else do any better.

I talked my buddy Craig Mathews into coming down and giving it a try. Either he wouldn't catch anything, and I would feel better about myself, or I would learn something from the master of stealth fishing.

He approached the stream cautiously as he spotted where the fish were swimming in the weed beds. He then sat down on the banks, feet in the water, and just observed what was going on. After a while, he began making short, accurate casts of no more line than double the length of his leader. He hooked several fish and landed three that day on his size 24 Sparkle Dun—the same fly I had been using.

The lesson: Trout that have been fished over a lot may not seem as skittish as wilder fish, but in shallow water their field of vision is almost 360 degrees. They see everything, and their response to seeing the angler is to keep their mouths shut to everything that is offered. It's not about the fly, but about the angler's approach. The knees and butt of your waders should wear out faster than the feet.

–Y.C.

Y.C. spring creek fishing, Patagonia. MAURO MAZZO

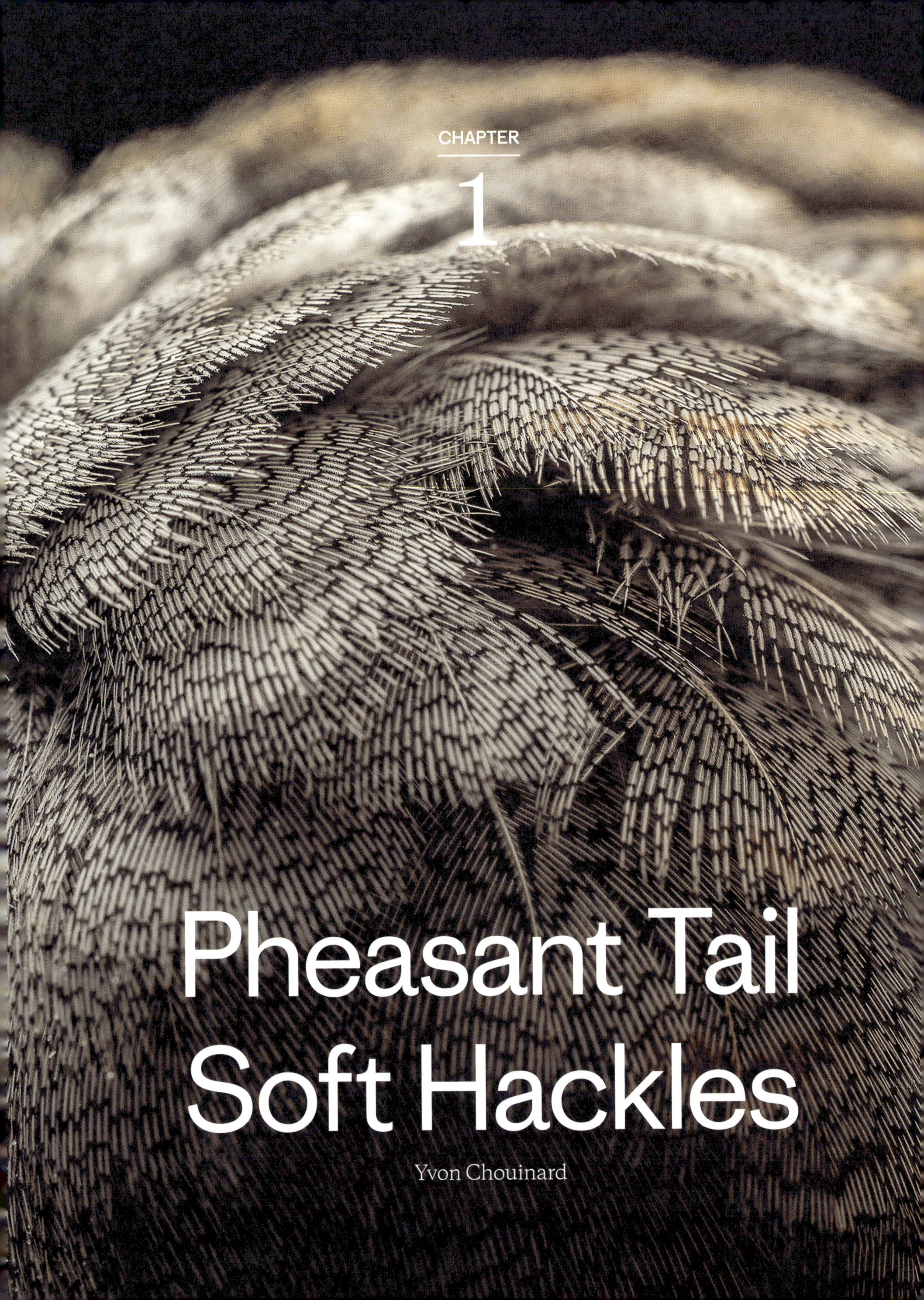

CHAPTER

1

Pheasant Tail Soft Hackles

Yvon Chouinard

What we have learned from years of fishing with long, flexible Tenkara rods, and with some minor modifications to the flies, is a method that is one of the most effective ways to catch fish. It is especially well suited to the beginner fly angler. We described this method in our book *Simple Fly Fishing.* But since our goal here is to keep the flies simple and allow us to focus on our skills, let's take it to the next level.

Soft-hackle wet flies—or spiders, as they're called in the United Kingdom—are among the oldest artificial flies, going back to at least the sixteenth century. They are elegant, use natural materials, and are simple to tie. They continue to fool fish today—oftentimes even better than the latest synthetic-material flies that populate modern fly-shop bins.

After reading the books of the Montana angler Sylvester Nemes, I started fishing soft hackles. The flies appealed to me because of their simplicity and versatility.

I started with two flies on my leader. Each one was a different size and color. I soon found that the Pheasant Tail and Partridge fly was outfishing all other versions and colors of the soft hackle. So, I thought, why not just stick with what works? Simple. I believe "he who dies with the least toys wins." By changing only the size and weight of the Pheasant Tail, I found that it imitates every stage of the mayfly, caddis, or stonefly. It's even the best bonefish fly I use.

In 2015, I fished in Europe, North and South America, and the Caribbean using only one type of fly—the Pheasant Tail and Partridge. I caught trout, grayling, salmon, steelhead, bonefish, and various other saltwater fish in numbers that exceeded what I'd done in other years. The most important lesson of this experiment is that without the distraction of changing fly patterns, I was free to focus on technique, depth, reading the water, and understanding what the fish were doing at any given time. Too often we anglers blame fly selection for the poor fishing when the truth is we are clueless about what is going on around us. It all starts with observation and technique.

Opposite: Hungarian partridge neck.

A STORY

Solving a Puzzle

One of the most memorable fish I've ever caught was on Flat Creek, which flows through the town of Jackson, Wyoming. It gets hit really hard, so the cutthroats are super wily. I fished over a large feeding fish for almost an hour with no success. I finally put it all together with a combination of 7X tippet, a difficult reach cast, and a stripped-down, size 22 Pale Morning Dun dry fly that I converted into a ragged, physically challenged emerger. The final piece of the puzzle was to put spittle on the tail end so that it floated at just the right angle in the surface film.

–Y.C.

A *Baetis* sparkle dun, a deadly mayfly pattern tied with a trailing shuck, imitates an impaired/crippled emerger caught in its nymphal shuck. FORREST MANKINS

Let's dig into the flies themselves, the techniques for fishing them, and some of the more unusual applications where they've been successful.

Selection and Use of Ring-Necked Pheasant Tail Feathers

The two long, center tail feathers are best to use when tying dry, wet, and nymph fly patterns. Each barb fiber from the stem (rachis) of these feathers is made up of tiny interlocking, frilly barbules that, when wrapped as fly bodies, create lifelike representations of trout-stream aquatic insects.

When you're tying dry flies, the frilly barbules readily accept dry-fly floatant, whether paste or liquid, so the fly floats like a cork when treated. After being taken by a fish or two, the fly can be renewed to float by dusting it with a dry-fly powder. If not treated with a floatant, these same barbules will absorb water and sink when used to tie wet flies and nymphs.

Simply stripping off, or clipping, the desired barbs from the stem and tying in with the thinner tips closest to the back of the fly will naturally create the proper taper and proportion of a natural insect. A general guide is to use four to eight barbs for fly bodies sizes 8 to 12, three or four barbs for sizes 14 to 16, and one or two barbs for sizes 20 and smaller. This is a general guide, as tail fibers vary from bird to bird, so the number of barbs and frilly fibers can vary as well. Don't be afraid to use more or fewer barbs to achieve the proper proportions for your flies.

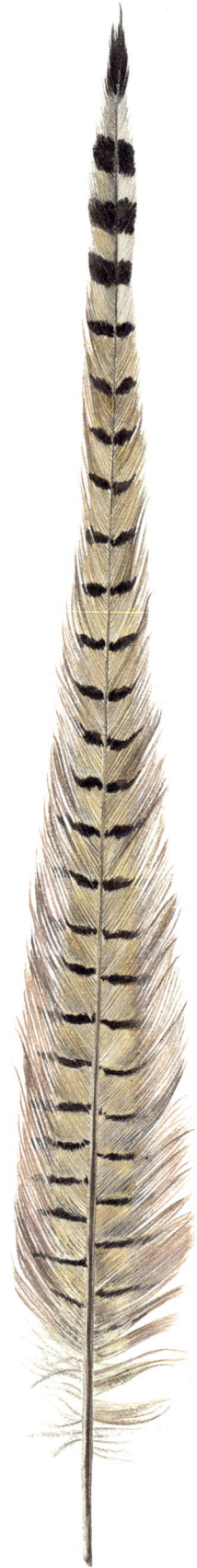

One of two center tail feathers from a rooster ringed-neck pheasant.

Selection and Use of Hungarian Partridge Feathers

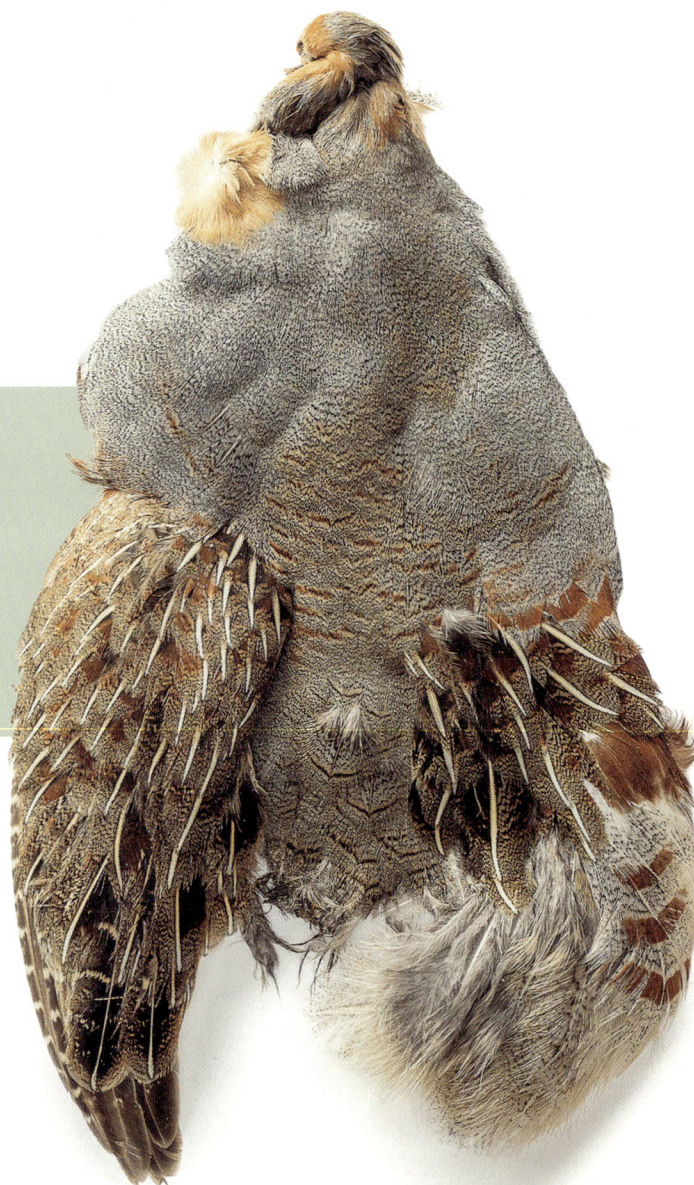

For tying proper soft-hackle flies, we recommend investing in an entire wild Hungarian partridge skin. You can expect to tie hundreds of flies from a single wild bird skin. We do not recommend buying a game-farm bird or purchasing a package of feathers. You will discover that domestic, pen-raised birds, and most feathers stuffed into plastic bags, offer only damaged, broken, and pecked fibers that render most feathers unusable. Pen-raised, tame Hungarian partridges, usually crammed into tiny quarters, fight constantly to establish their pecking order, which results in damaged feathers.

When searching for the best skin and feathers to tie soft hackles, look for one taken in late fall that offers clean, undamaged feathers in a variety of colors. Most skins will give fly tiers hundreds of light-gray mottled feathers along with brown, reddish, and golden-brown feathers.

We use all feathers from a Hungarian partridge skin for our soft hackles. Beginning at the head of the bird, expect to find small, well-mottled feathers for smaller flies. Moving down to the throat of the bird skin and along the sides, look for the well-marked gray feathers that we use on most soft-hackle patterns. Next, from the throat and sides of the skin to the back of the bird and down to the tail, you'll find hundreds of large, well-mottled brown, golden, and tan feathers used for several soft-hackle patterns and especially for bonefish flies.

A wild Hungarian partridge cape. Its perfectly mottled and shaded feathers will tie hundreds of soft hackles.

Fishing the Flymph

This soft-hackle fly, tied on a heavier hook, is really a combination nymph and emerger. It was called a Flymph by James Leisenring and Pete Hidy in their books *The Art of Tying the Wet Fly* and *Fishing the Flymph*. Their technique is to simply cast across and up a bit to let the fly sink deeply. When the line straightens downstream, lift the rod to bring the fly to the surface. This simple action is the Leisenring Lift. Most times the fish will take as the *lift* pulls the fly toward the surface. If you try to do this with a fly tied on a light hook, it will drag on the surface, which often produces the same effect as any other dragging dry fly—a refusal.

The Gear for Flymphs

I now do almost all my trout fishing with either an eight-foot, three-weight cane rod or a ten-foot, two-weight nymphing rod. The light rods allow me to better impart action with the flexible tip. A stiff five-weight rod, after you cast, is just a stick in your hand. Also, the lighter two- and three-weight lines help avoid the line droop that comes off the end of the rod. You want a tight connection from the tip of your rod to the fly. I also use hand-knotted leaders, which create more drag in the water, further straightening the line and providing the all-important direct connection to the fly. Then add a four-foot tippet of 4X or 5X. The lighter the tippet, the deeper the fly will sink. The combination of a light, flexible rod; a narrow, light line; and a hand-knotted leader makes the following technique possible.

Upper Madison River, Yellowstone National Park.
RICH CROWDER

Line Droop: When fishing flymphs, stiff rods and heavy lines (e.g. five-weight) should be avoided. A stiff rod will be unable to impart action on the flies, and the heavy line will droop off the rod tip, reducing the connection to the flies.

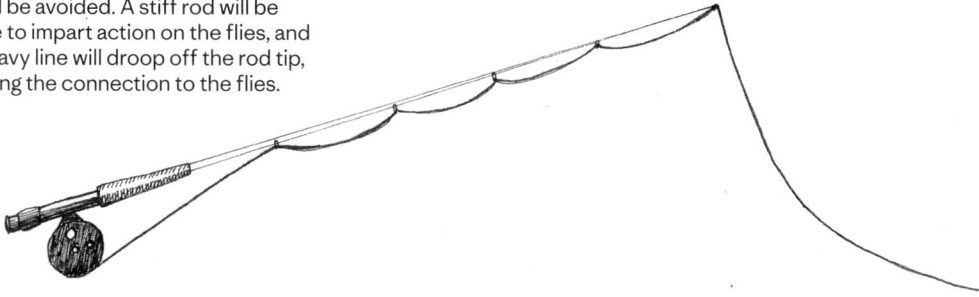

No Line Droop: Lighter fly rods and lines (e.g. two- or three-weight) will help avoid line droop and will provide a direct connection between the rod and flies. The flexible tip of these light rods will help to better impart action on the flies.

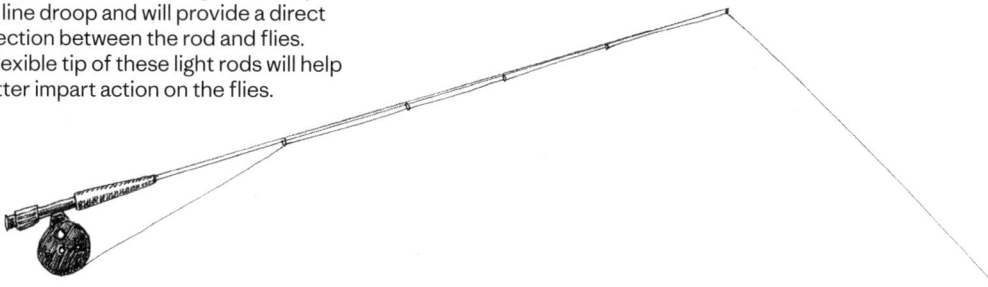

With a two-fly system, I recommend having the larger fly on the point and one size smaller on the dropper. I tie the dropper on the tag end of a surgeon's knot and keep the flies about three to four feet apart. The reason for fishing two flies, besides giving the trout a choice of different sizes, is that they will have different actions. At times I've caught eight out of ten fish on the dropper fly, at other times the opposite. Be warned: Fishing with two flies is illegal in some places around the world.

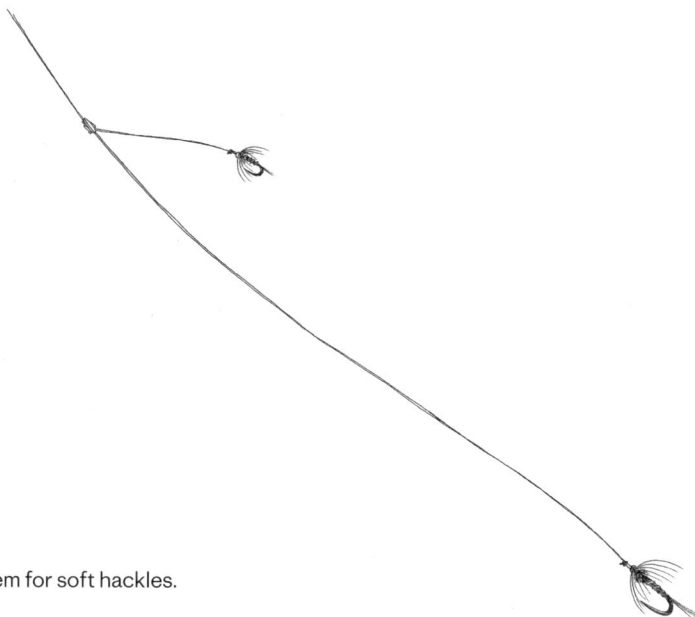

The two-fly system for soft hackles.

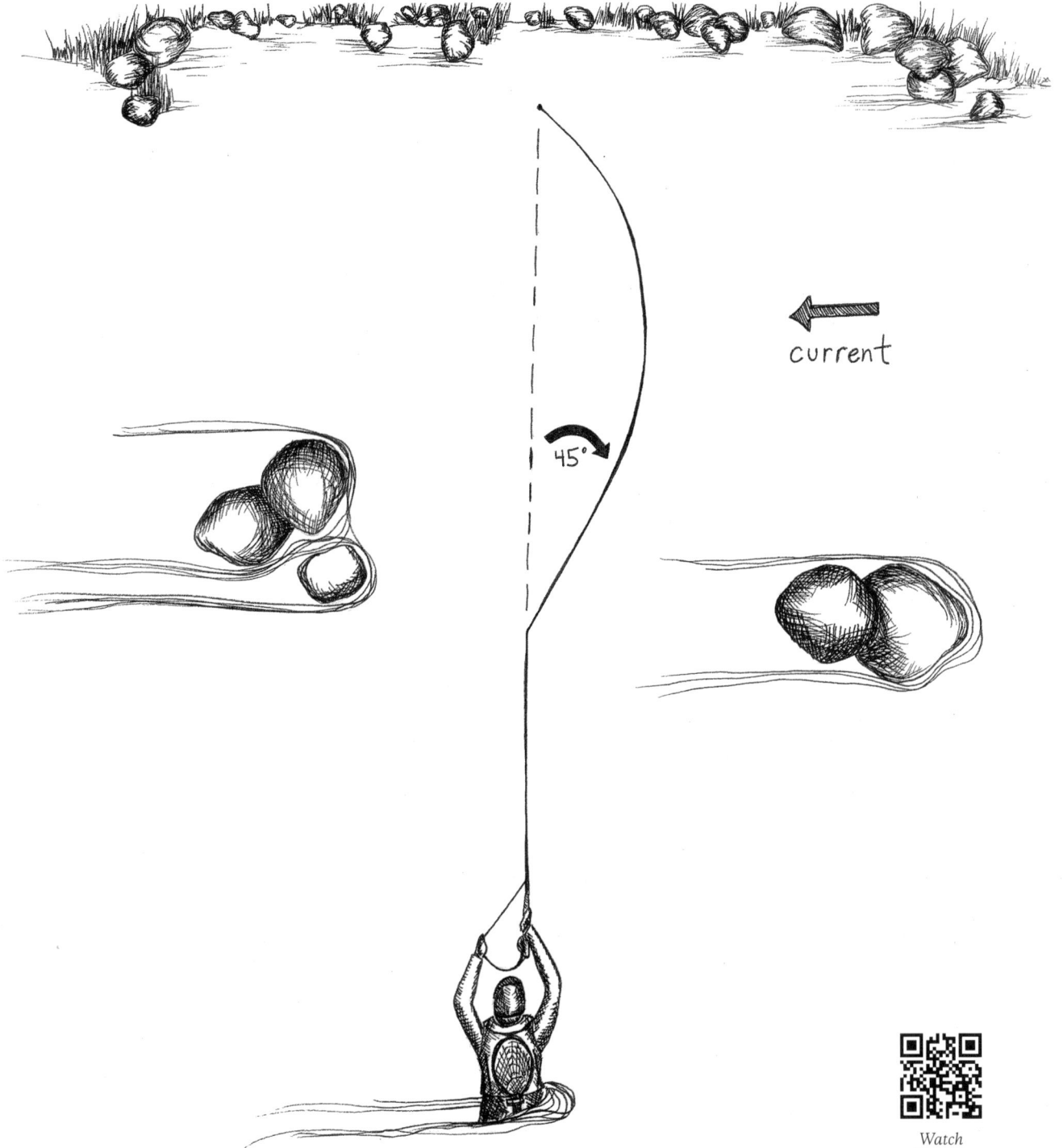

current

45°

The upstream mend.

Cast the line across the current at about a forty-five-degree angle downstream. As soon as the fly is in the water, lift the slack part of your line and place it to the side and slightly upstream.

This upstream mend slows the swing of the fly. Make sure you don't over-mend and pull the fly out of the water. The upstream mend also prevents the slack line from getting caught by the current, resulting in your fly swinging at an unnaturally fast speed. It also gives time for the fly to sink. The ten-foot rod makes mending easier.

With your rod at about a twenty-degree angle down to the water, follow the line with the tip of the rod. As the line tightens, lift the rod tip to about a thirty-five-degree angle. (Don't worry if you left your protractor at home—your angles don't need to be exact.) As the fly swings, make an occasional twitch with the tip of the rod. It's important that the tip moves only two or three inches at most, no more.

To make the proper twitch, hold the rod with your thumb on the top of the handle and your upper arm straight down in a relaxed position (easy on the rotator cuff). The twitch is imparted to the tip by squeezing the bottom fingers of the hand, not by raising the rod.

If you look at your hand while you are doing this, you hardly see any movement at all. Almost everyone who tries to do this twitch overdoes it at first. Here's the rule: If you think you're not moving the fly enough, move it less. The key is to work only the top foot and a half of the rod, and just squeezing those bottom two fingers does the trick beautifully.

What you're trying to do is imitate the emerging and swimming stages of the caddis or mayfly. This is the stage when they are most vulnerable to trout. As a result of the twitching actions, the Flymph is moving upward through the water in tiny increments of one to three inches. While it may resemble the traditional wet-fly swing, what we're doing here is quite different—and far more effective.

Note: If you don't fish with the light rods mentioned earlier, you can still approximate the twitching technique. Just place the rod tip down to the water and strip in line in two- or three-inch increments. On lakes or on extremely windy days, you may even need to do this with the two- or three-weight rods to keep a straight line and direct connection to the fly.

If I were limited to trout fishing with only one pattern of fly, I would choose a size 14 Pheasant Tail Flymph in the spring and early summer and a size 16 or 18 in the midsummer and fall.

Watch the video: How to fish a flymph

A STORY

Fishing the Spatsizi

I was fishing in the Spatsizi Wilderness of British Columbia, the headwaters of the Skeena and Stikine Rivers. Most of the rainbows and bull trout in this extremely remote place had never seen a fly before. On my last day I stood in one place and caught thirty fat rainbows using a Pheasant Tail Flymph. Then I realized I had been fishing for an indeterminate amount of time with no fly left on the hook. It didn't matter; as long as I did the emerger twitch, the fish took the bare hook. That proved, once again, it's the action that counts.

–Y.C.

Spatsizi Wilderness, British Columbia.
GARY FIEGEHEN / ALL CANADA
PHOTOS / SUPERSTOCK

Pheasant Tail

Wet Fly Patterns

Pheasant Tail
Flymph

Pheasant Tail
Bead Head Flymph

Classic Pheasant Tail
Soft Hackle

Pheasant Tail
Soft Hackle Dry Fly

Pheasant Tail
Trico Spinner

Angler Y.C. RICH CROWDER

Pheasant Tail

Flymph

Using partridge feathers from the head and neck of a good cape, you can tie soft-hackle patterns down to about size 24. For smaller patterns, you can use hen feathers or coverlet feathers from various ducks and game birds. Also, don't waste a tweety bird hit by a car or one that hit a window.

Don't worry if your fly doesn't look perfect. With Flymphs, it's the action that counts.

MATERIALS

Hook: Umpqua UC610BL-BN, 1X heavy, wide gap, barbless, #8–#20

Thread: 8/0 Semperfli, olive

Ribbing: Extra-small to medium gold copper wire

Tail: 4-8 pheasant tail barbs (4 for #14)

Body: Pheasant tail barbs used for tail

Thorax: Hareline Hare'e Ice Dub, peacock

Hackle: Gray Hungarian partridge

Watch the step-by-step video

35

.01 Begin by tying in the working thread just behind the eye of the hook. Tie on the wire rib and then wrap the thread back to the bend of the shank.

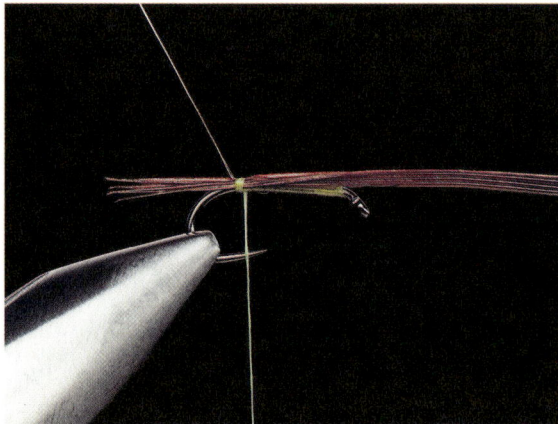

.02 Tie in four to eight pheasant tail barbs to form the tail, 1/8" to 1/4" long (1/4" for #14).

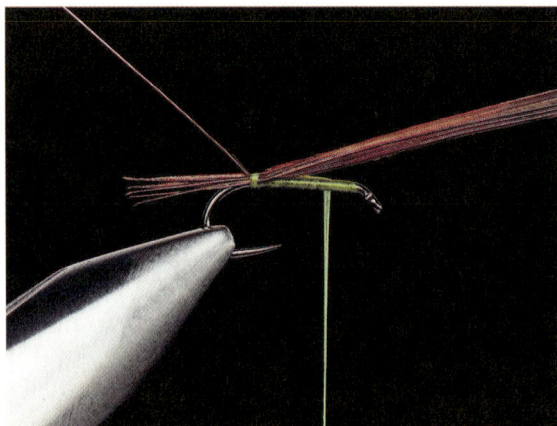

.03 Wrap the thread two-thirds of the way up the hook.

.04 Wrap the pheasant tail barbs with the thread to form the abdomen. Tie off and trim the butts.

.05 Wrap the wire ribbing forward three or four times to reinforce the pheasant tail abdomen. Tie off and trim the wire rib.

.06 Dub a thorax of peacock Hare'e Ice Dub, leaving room to tie in and wrap the hackle. (The Ice Dub thorax creates air bubbles that imitate the bubbles of emerging caddis or mayflies. We believe this is an important trigger to further entice the fish.)

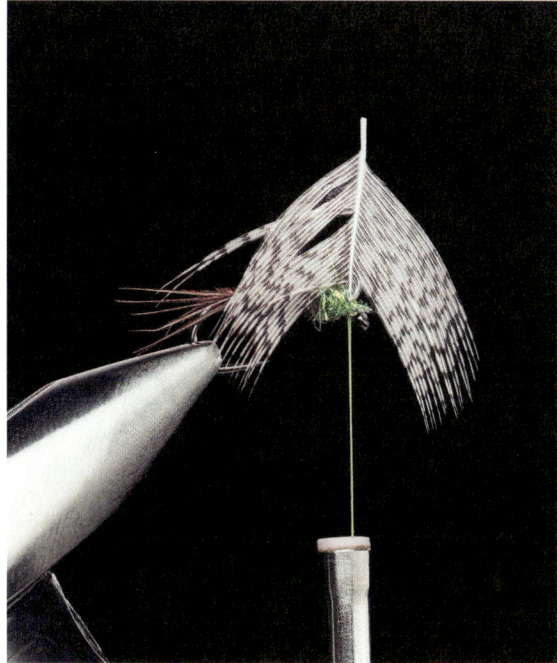

.07 Select a gray Hungarian partridge hackle with fibers just longer than the hook shank and tie in the tip with the concave side of the feather facing up toward you.

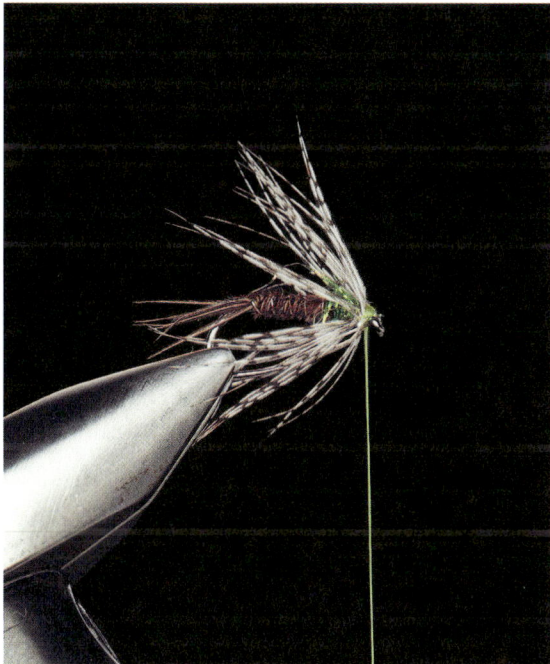

.08 Wrap the hackle twice, then tie off and trim.

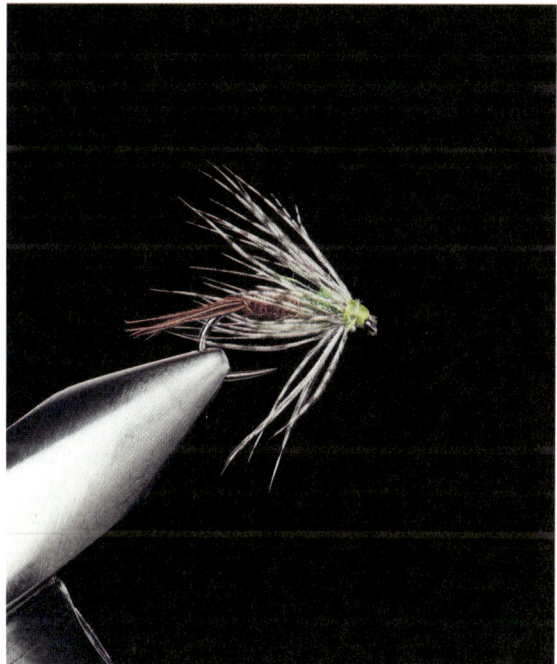

.09 Take a couple thread wraps through the hackle to strengthen. Whip finish.

Pheasant Tail

Bead Head Flymph

This fly—which is the same pattern as the Flymph, but with a bead added—can be fished like the Flymph, with the advantage that it sinks deeper. It can also be fished like a nymph.

MATERIALS

Hook: Umpqua UC610BL-BN, #10–#18

Bead: Black brass bead (7/64 inch for #12)

Thread: 8/0 Semperfli, olive

Ribbing: Extra-small to small gold copper wire

Tail: 4-8 pheasant tail barbs (4 for #14)

Body: Pheasant tail barbs used for tail

Thorax: Hareline Hare'e Ice Dub, peacock

Hackle: Gray Hungarian partridge

The steps to tie this fly are the same as for the Pheasant Tail Flymph but with a bead added at the beginning of Step 1. Reference the step-by-step recipe and the QR code to an instructional video for the Flymph on page 35.

Y.C. fly fishing in Patagonia, Argentina.
BRYAN GREGSON

Classic Pheasant Tail
Soft Hackle

The Pheasant Tail Soft Hackle—which is the same as a Flymph—is normally tied on a dry-fly hook. It can be greased with floatant and fished as you would any dry fly. The floating Pheasant Tail Soft Hackle will not float very high on the surface like a true dry Adams or Light Cahill because of its soft hackles. Actually, that's the good news because it more closely imitates a mayfly or caddis in trouble.

We know that trout take 90 percent of their food under the surface of the water. What we often perceive as a fish rising to duns on the surface is only correct about 5 percent of the time. If a trout sees a dun mayfly drifting on the surface drying its wings, it knows there's a good chance the mayfly will fly off before the trout can sip it in. Trout are masters of not wasting energy chasing such a low-calorie proposition. That's why they prefer to pick on the most vulnerable stages of aquatic insects: a nymph or caddis pupa, an emerger, a physically challenged fly trapped in its shuck, or even easier, a stillborn fly floating just under the surface.

During a hatch, if you're getting refusals with your dry fly, go smaller. If that doesn't work, try an emerger, nymph, soft hackle, or Flymph. Often one of these variations is more likely to work than continuously trying various dry flies.

Without the floatant, the soft-hackle fly will sink slightly below the surface. The *drowned* soft hackle, drifting in the surface film, is even a good imitation of a spent spinner.

MATERIALS

Hook: Umpqua UC600BN-BL, dry fly, wide gap, #10–#20; Tiemco TMC 100BL, #22–#24

Thread: 8/0 Semperfli, olive

Ribbing: Thread

Tail: 2-8 pheasant tail barbs (4 for #14)

Body: Pheasant tail barbs used for tail

Thorax: Semperfli Kapok Dubbing, olive

Hackle: Gray Hungarian partridge

The steps to tie this fly are the same as for the Pheasant Tail Flymph but with a different hook and different dubbing. Reference the step-by-step recipe and the QR code to an instructional video for the Flymph on page 35.

Y.C. on the Babine River, British Columbia.
DAVE PAGE

Pheasant Tail

Soft Hackle Dry Fly

This version of the soft hackle was first introduced in England in the mid-1800s. It is tied to float higher on the water than the normal soft hackle, where it imitates the dun or spinner stage of mayflies.

MATERIALS

Hook: Umpqua UC600-BN, dry fly, #10–#20; Tiemco TMC 100BL, #22–#24

Thread: 8/0 Semperfli, olive

Ribbing: Thread

Tail: 2-6 pheasant tail barbs (4 for #14)

Body: Pheasant tail barbs used for tail

Rooster hackle: Your choice of color

Soft hackle: Gray Hungarian partridge, hackle should extend to bend of hook

Watch the step-by-step video

.01 Begin by wrapping the working thread on the hook shank, leaving the tag end untrimmed and two to three inches long beyond the bend of the hook. This will become the ribbing. Select two to six pheasant tail barbs and tie them in as tails (1/4" long), leaving the ends untrimmed. Now, wrap the fibers forward two-thirds of the way up the hook shank to form the abdomen, then tie off and trim the ends.

.02 With the tag end of the working thread left at the tie-in point of the tails, wrap forward four to five times over the pheasant tail fibers used to form the fly body. This reinforces the pheasant tail fibers. Tie in the rooster hackle.

.03 Wrap the rooster hackle forward three or four turns. You can use any color rooster hackle you wish. For example, use dun for Baetis, or cream for Pale Morning Duns.

48

.04   Next, tie in the soft Hungarian partridge hackle in front of the rooster hackle.

.05   Wrap the Hungarian partridge hackle one or two turns. Make sure you push the hackle tight. This helps keep the hackle "open," so it doesn't lie down along the hook shank. Tie off and trim the excess hackle and whip finish.

Pheasant Tail
Trico Spinner

Fishing the Trico hatch can drive you crazy. If you are not out at dawn when these tiny flies hatch, you are doomed to fish the clouds and rafts of the spinner fall, hoping a fish will take your fly over the thousands of naturals.

I created this pattern, which works for the emerger stage and the spent spinner. It is fished with the tiniest of twitches to differentiate itself from the millions of dead, still naturals on the water. Only two materials (pheasant tail fibers and white hen hackle) are needed to tie this simple and effective Trico mayfly spinner pattern.

MATERIALS

Hook: Tiemco TMC 2488, dry fly, #20–#24

Thread: 12/0 Semperfli, black

Tail: 2 white hen hackle barbs

Abdomen: 1-2 pheasant tail barbs

Thorax: Pheasant tail barbs used for abdomen

Hackle: Two turns of white hen hackle

Watch the step-by-step video

51

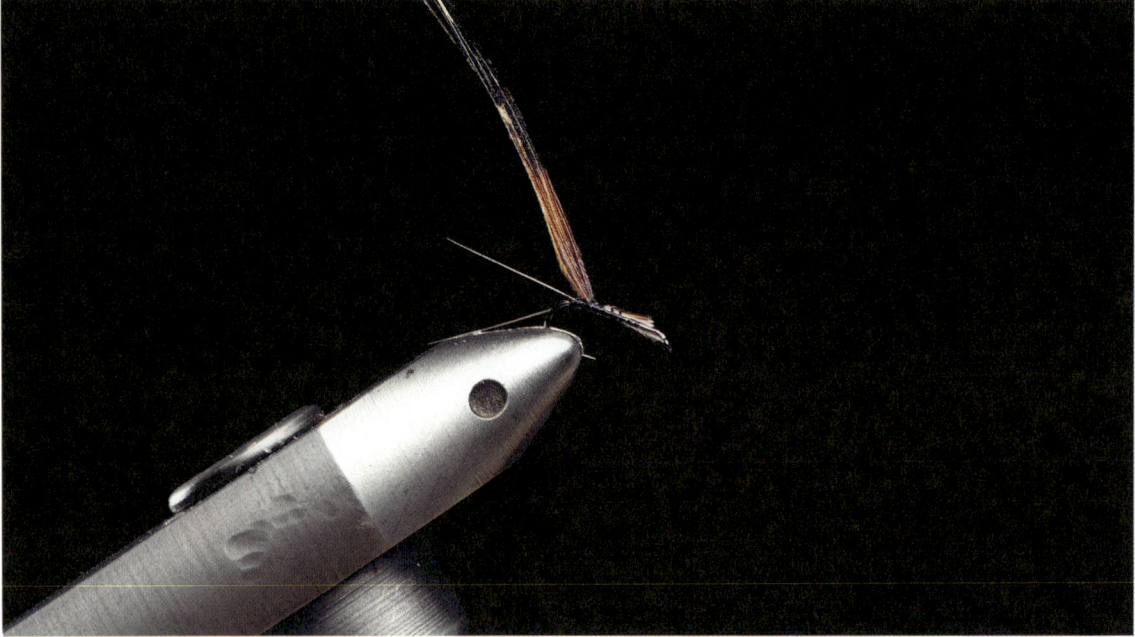

.01   Begin by tying in the working thread above the bend of the hook, and then tie in two split barbs of the hen hackle to form the tails. The tails should be three to four times the length of the hook shank. Tie in two to three pheasant tail barbs by the tips.

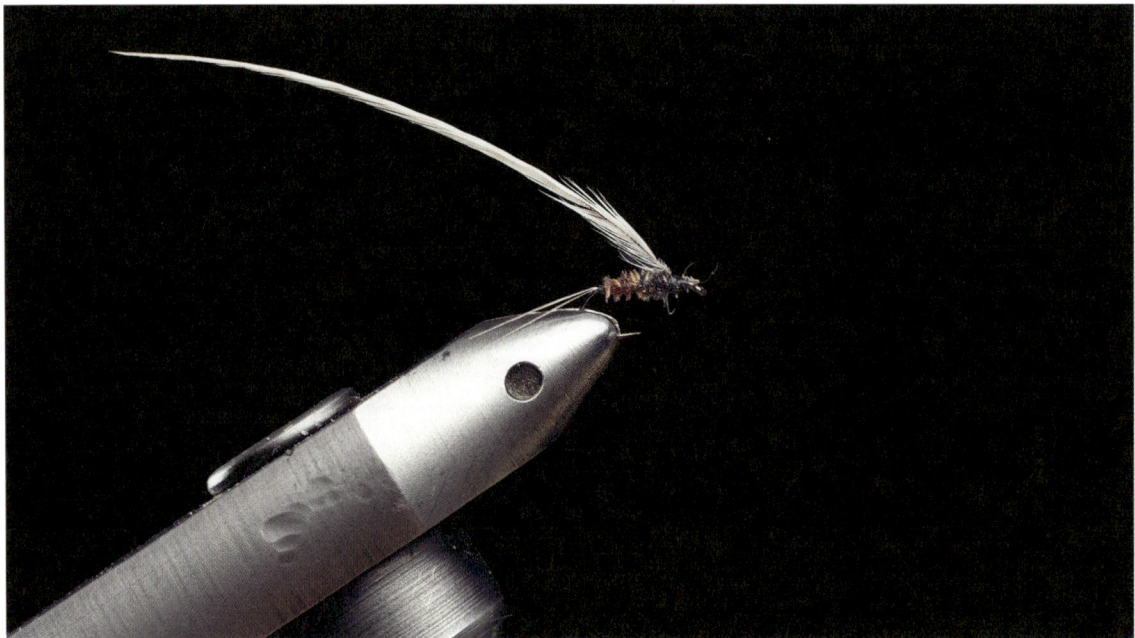

.02   Wrap the pheasant tail barbs forward two-thirds of the way up the hook shank to form a tapered abdomen and thorax. Next, tie in a white hen hackle.

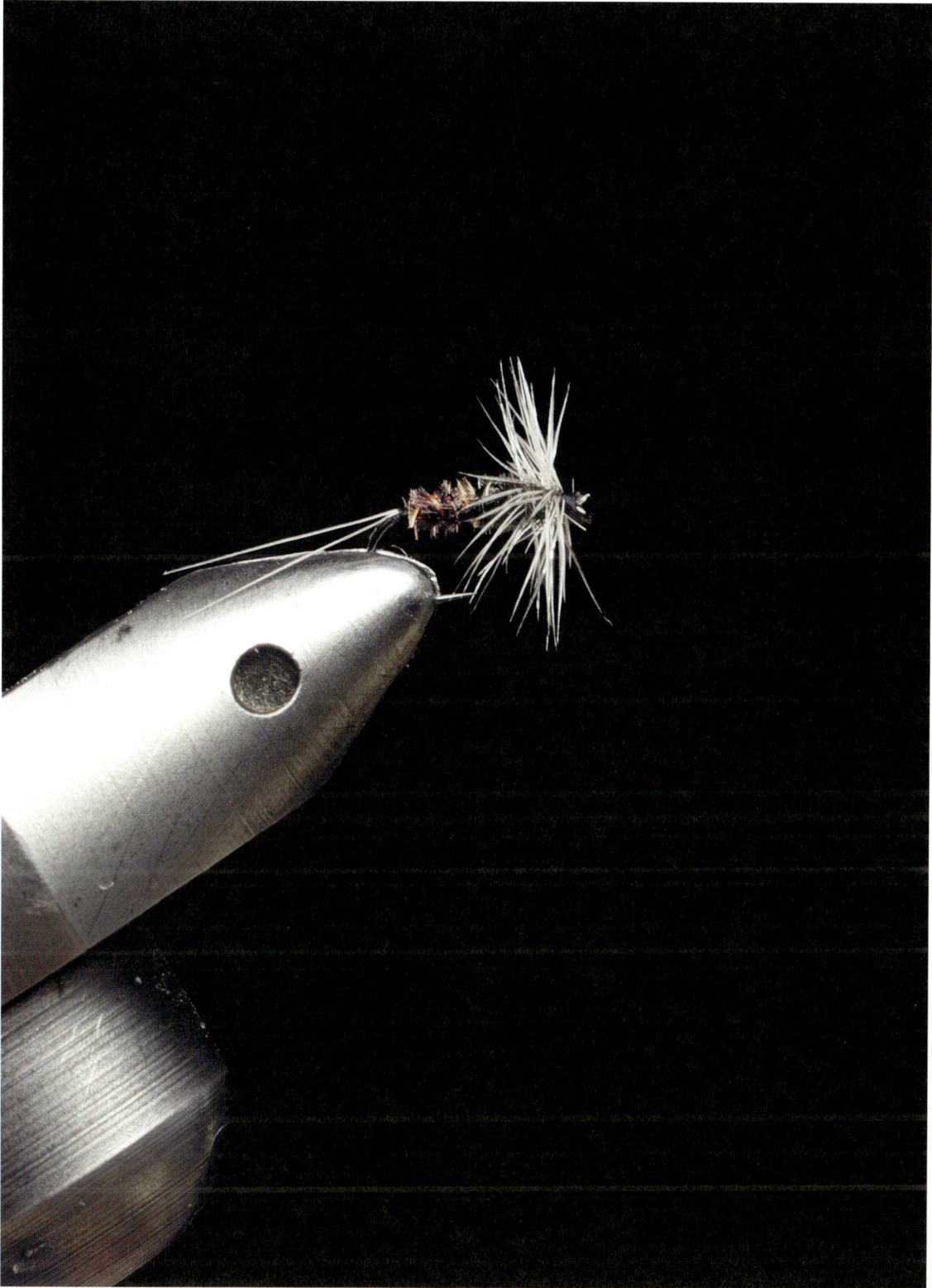

.03 Take two to three turns of the white hen hackle in front of the thorax, and tie off behind the eye of the hook. Whip finish.

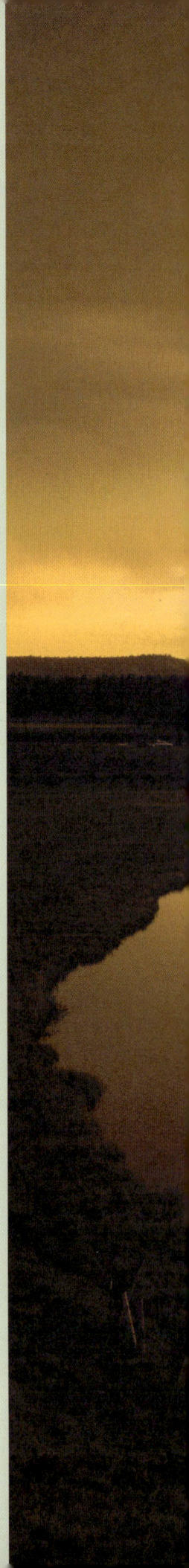

A STORY

Railroad
Ranch Tricos

I showed up at Idaho's Railroad Ranch and asked friends and hot locals Nelson Ishiyama and Bruce Raskin what was going on. "Well," they said, "the good news is they are taking Tricos. The bad news is they are focused on the pregnant females, which have a tiny black dot on their rears."

-Y.C.

Sunset. Henry's Fork, Idaho. RICH CROWDER

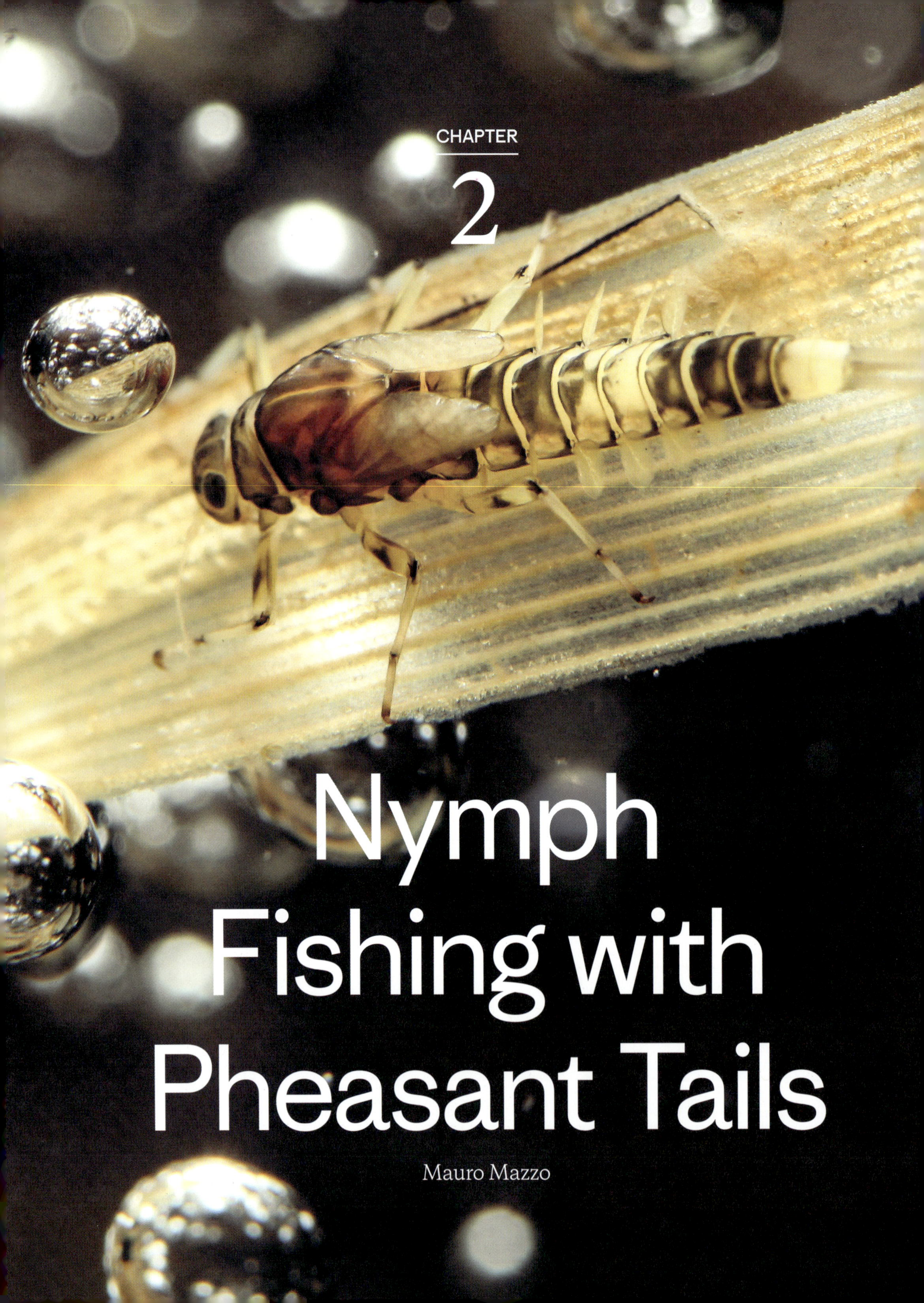

CHAPTER

2

Nymph Fishing with Pheasant Tails

Mauro Mazzo

In traditional Italian cooking we say, "five ingredients, no more." This is the standard by which a cook's proficiency and the resulting quality of a dish are judged. While it may seem like an arbitrary and overly stringent constraint, it serves an important purpose: It means each of the five chosen ingredients (of course, olive oil and spices don't count) must be perfect, and they need to be combined with the utmost skill. Limiting your options, whether in cooking or fishing, forces creativity and learning. Do it right and you can achieve spectacular results. Discovery and practice, and then mastery and perfection, all through simplification: Isn't that the goal of practicing any craft?

The art of nymphing is like fishing blind. The action is going on beneath the surface. Like a burglar cracking a safe, it's all about concentration and feel, rather than sight. The angler must be aware of the speed of the flowing water on the surface *and* on the bottom. You must visualize the path of the unseen nymph and guess if it will entice a fish enough to take it.

The specific nymph pattern sometimes matters, but the angler's skill is paramount. Learning to fish properly one style of fly in different sizes and weights will always be more effective than relying on boxes of hundreds of different flies.

The advantage of fishing with nymphs is you don't need a hatch. If you present your fly, lifelike and close to the fish's mouth, the fish will take it. That's why everyone in international fishing competitions fishes mainly with nymphs.

In this chapter, I am not going to attempt to teach you the basics of how to fish. I assume you already know how. I will describe the flies I use and give you a few tips on simplifying your gear, and hopefully give you the confidence that with just a few flies, you can cover most situations.

Opposite: Mayfly nymph clinging to a blade of dead grass in a trout stream. TROUTFODDER / ADOBE STOCK

Above: No need for a head net. Mauro Mazzo in Labrador. YVON CHOUINARD

A STORY

Grayling
with a Friend

I was fishing for grayling with a good friend on one of my favorite rivers, the Passirio near Merano, Italy. It was a very cold late-autumn day and there was no hope for a hatch. I was fishing a small nymph. After half an hour, I caught the first grayling and then proceeded to catch a few more. My friend was fishing the opposite bank, and by the time I had covered forty feet, he had already fished his way more than two hundred feet upstream. After watching me land several fish, he came back and shouted across the water, "Mauro, what fly are you using?" I yelled back, "The P.T. with orange thorax." He answered, "Impossible, I am fishing the same fly and did not catch a single fish."

I demonstrated that I was fishing very slowly, trying to cover every inch of water, knowing that with the cold temperature, the fish would not move very far for my nymph. I suggested that he make short, accurate casts, close to each other, not more than a foot apart. He followed my advice and after a few casts, he got his first fish. By the end of the day, he had landed several nice grayling.

It was the technique that made the difference.

–M.M.

Grayling dorsals catching every angle of light.
STEVEN G. GNAM

Nymphing Gear

Rod and Reel

Even though the trend today is toward longer rods for nymphing, any two- to four-weight rod from nine to ten feet is fine. A progressive action with a sensitive tip provides an advantage for giving action to the nymph and avoiding breakoffs with large fish and light tippets.

A large-arbor reel that balances well with the rod is important because high-stick nymphing all day with an unbalanced outfit will eventually blow out your rotator cuff. Trust me on this.

Flies

The Classic Pheasant Tail Nymph is meant to be fished near the top of the water column. It's a good fly to use as a first dropper under an indicator or large dry fly. Bead head nymphs on straight hooks are fished at midlevel or near the bottom. Flies tied on grub and jig hooks are good as point flies because they will bounce along the bottom and reduce snag possibilities. *Note:* If you use jig hooks, do not tie them as droppers; they will spin around, twisting the line.

To make flies sink faster, use tungsten bead heads or twist some tin or copper wire around the hook before tying it. Lead, which is toxic to aquatic life and waterfowl in all its forms—sinker, split shot, or lead wire—has no place in any responsible freshwater angler's kit.

Be careful not to overweight your flies. The lighter the fly, the better the action will be. To increase the sinking rate, tie them with a slim body.

When fishing deep pools, casting farther upstream with a tuck or an S cast will allow more time for the fly to sink.

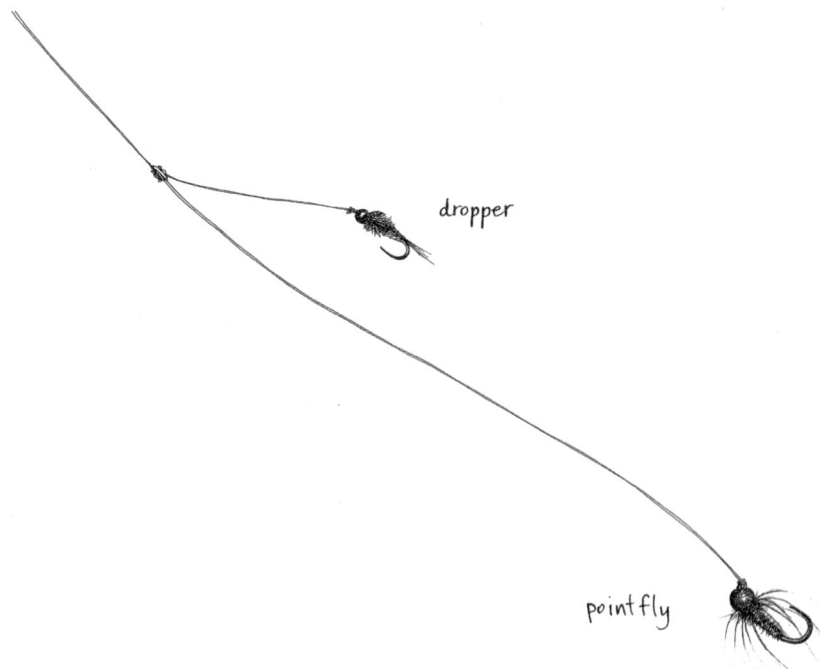

dropper

point fly

The two-fly system for nymphs.

Grayling and a cripple. Wind River, Yukon.
PETER MATHER

Line   I use a monofilament line that is 0.010 to 0.015 inch (0.25 to 0.35 mm) thick and sixty feet long, and attach it to the end of my fly line (A, below). It's a very effective setup, especially in the wind. It can be a bother to cast if you're not used to it. Instead, you may want to use a fine diameter Euro nymph fly line that's also good in the wind and easier to cast (B). A last-minute solution: Simply remove the tapered leader from a regular floating line and replace it with straight monofilament. Adjust the length depending on the depth of the water. Then use the end of your fly line as the indicator. This will work fine for short-distance nymphing. With this option (C), a two- or three-weight line is preferable.

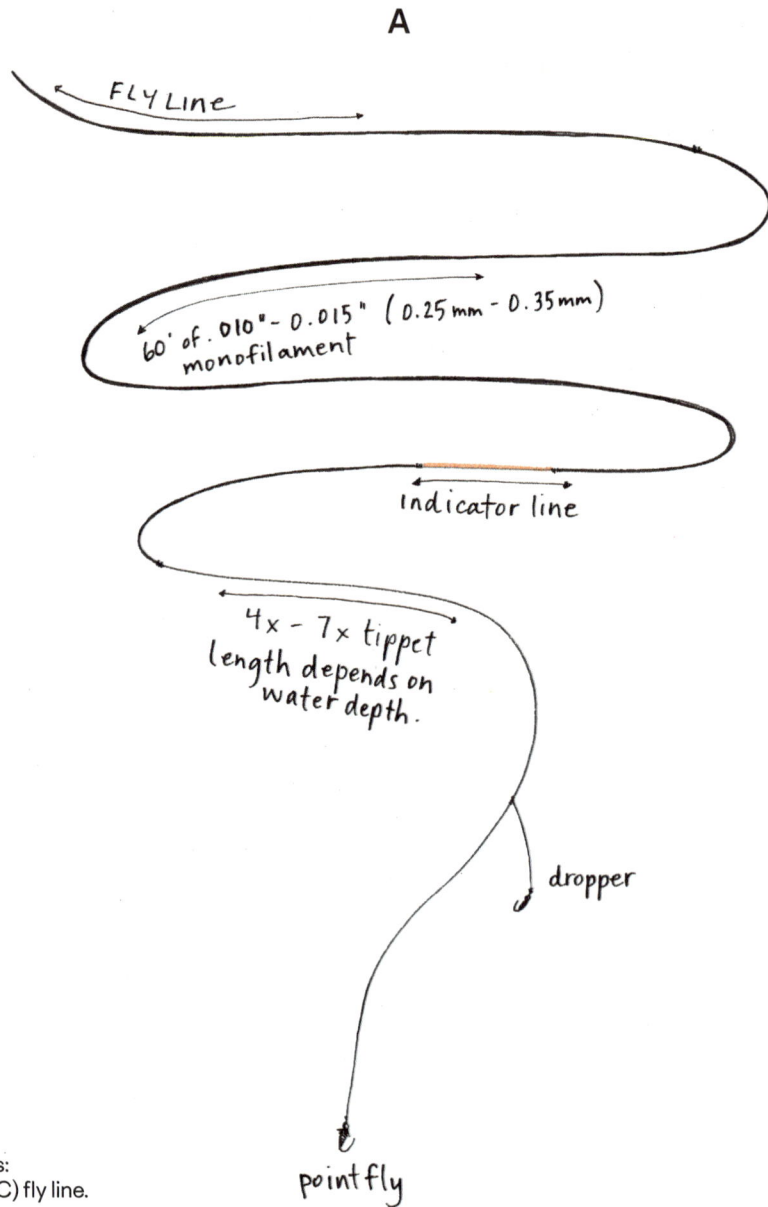

A

FLY Line

60' of .010"- 0.015" (0.25 mm - 0.35 mm) monofilament

Indicator line

4x - 7x tippet length depends on water depth.

dropper

point fly

Three different leader set-ups:
A) mono, B) Euro nymph line, C) fly line.

Leader

Forget about all the so-called magic leader formulas for the Polish, Spanish, Czech, French, or whatever techniques. On the fly end of whatever line or monofilament you use, just tie one foot of high-visibility fluorescent nylon that will act as an indicator, then a straight tippet of 4X to 7X. The tippet should be about one and a half times longer than the water is deep. The thinner the tippet, the faster the flies will sink and the less they will be affected by the current.

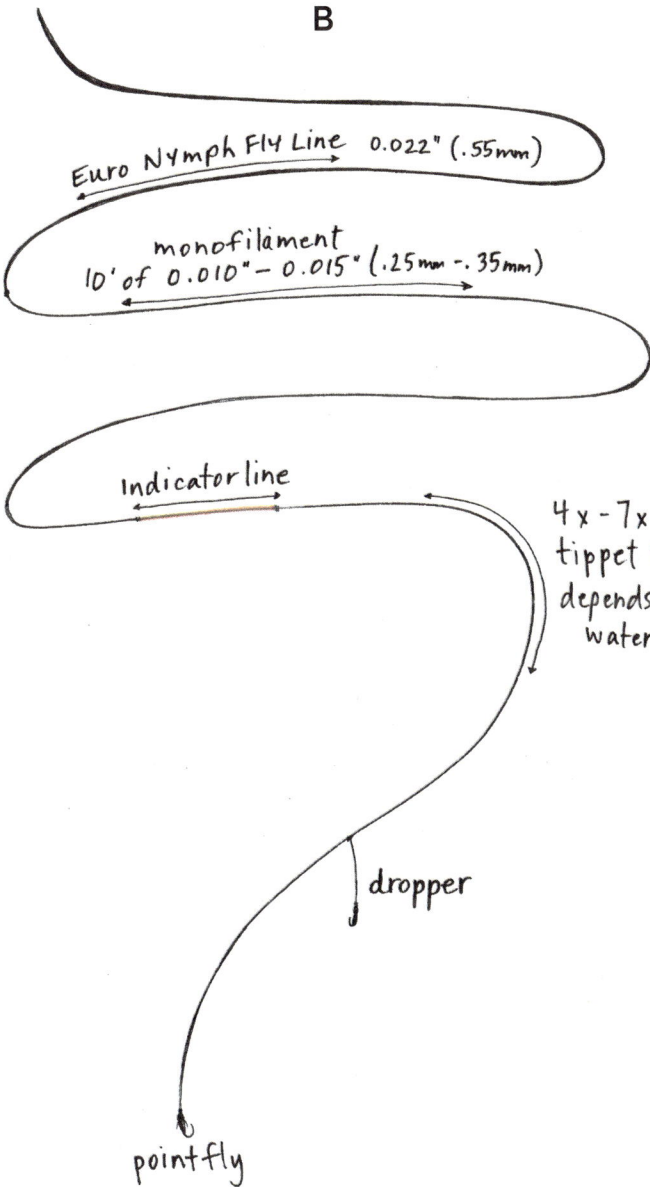

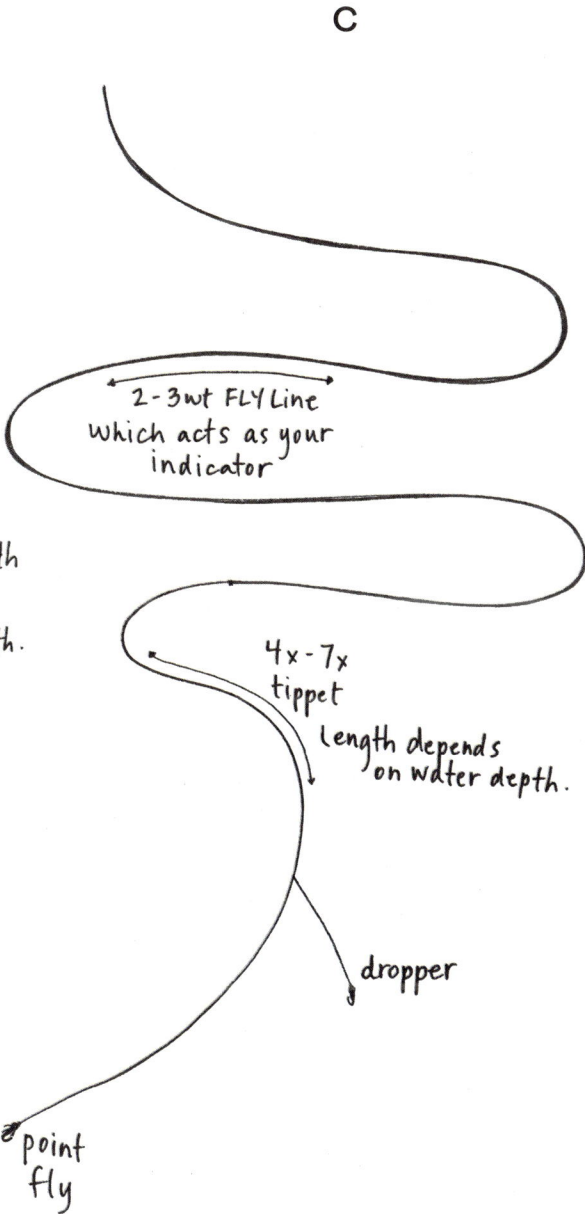

B

Euro Nymph Fly Line 0.022" (.55mm)

monofilament
10' of 0.010" – 0.015" (.25mm -.35mm)

Indicator line

4x – 7x tippet length depends on water depth.

dropper

point fly

C

2-3wt Fly Line which acts as your indicator

4x – 7x tippet length depends on water depth.

dropper

point fly

63

Technique

The first thing to understand is the speed of the current. You want your nymphs to drift at the same speed or slower than the water is moving. Natural insects do not drift faster than the current, and an artificial nymph speeding along is as much a turnoff for an educated trout as drag on a dry fly. Imagine the leader or tippet using the water current (as a sail uses the wind) to increase the nymph's speed.

To visualize the speed of the current, study the bubbles, foam, or floating debris going by. They indicate the speed of the water on the surface of the stream. Remember, though, that the flow of the river is slower near the bottom. Do not use tapered leaders or a heavy tippet. They will pull along at the speed of the surface water, which is not what you want for a natural drift.

Floating in a boat with the angler using a nymph dropper one or two feet below the surface is easy and effective because the boat and indicator setup are all moving at the same speed as the current. It's the state of the art of guided fishing in the United States. But it's hardly fly fishing. In fact, it's no different than the way some of us learned to fish using a bamboo pole with a bobber and a worm. When you see the bobber go down, you set the hook. Easy. But don't get me wrong, the bobber, or indicator fly, can be a valuable tool in what is termed "Euro nymphing."

Managing the nymph so it drifts at the same speed as the current, and giving action to the fly so it looks like a living insect, is the art of modern nymphing.

When nymph fishing, always remember that the speed of the current is slower close to the bottom.

Watch the video: How to fish a nymph

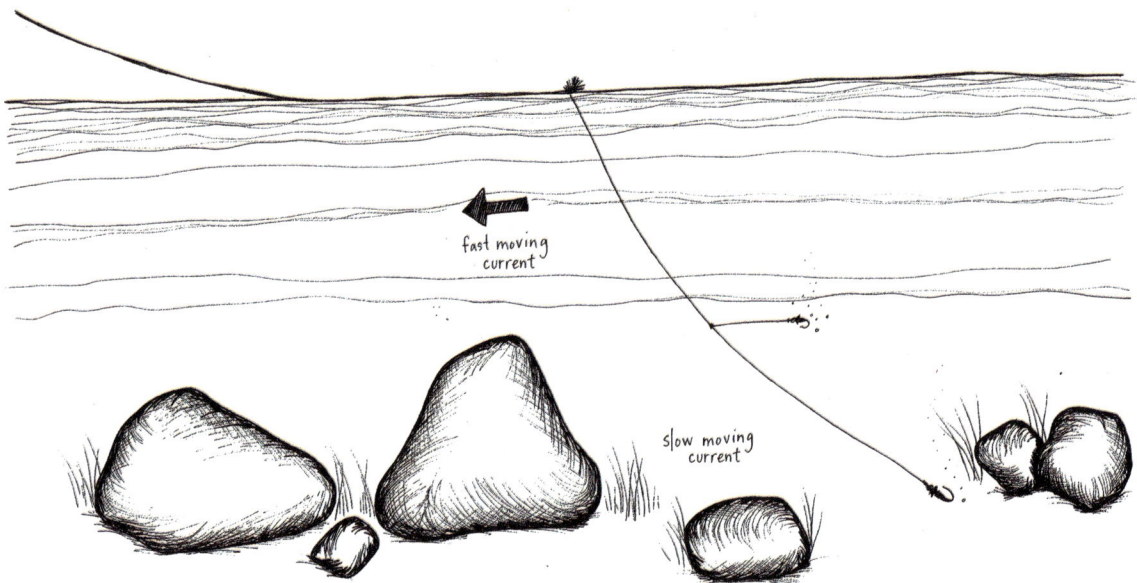

fast moving current

slow moving current

Short-Distance Nymphing

When fishing at short distances, there's no advantage to using a nymphing versus a monofilament line. In most cases, you will have only the leader out of the guides anyway. If you're using two flies, keep the dropper close to the point fly—about ten to fifteen inches works beautifully. Put the heavier fly on the point. This doesn't require casting skill; just lob the nymphs upstream at an angle close to the bank to make the flies sink quickly. When you think the flies are close to the bottom, start making small twitches with the tip of the rod for the entire length of the drift. This has a dual purpose: It prevents snagging on the bottom and gives a lifelike action to the fly.

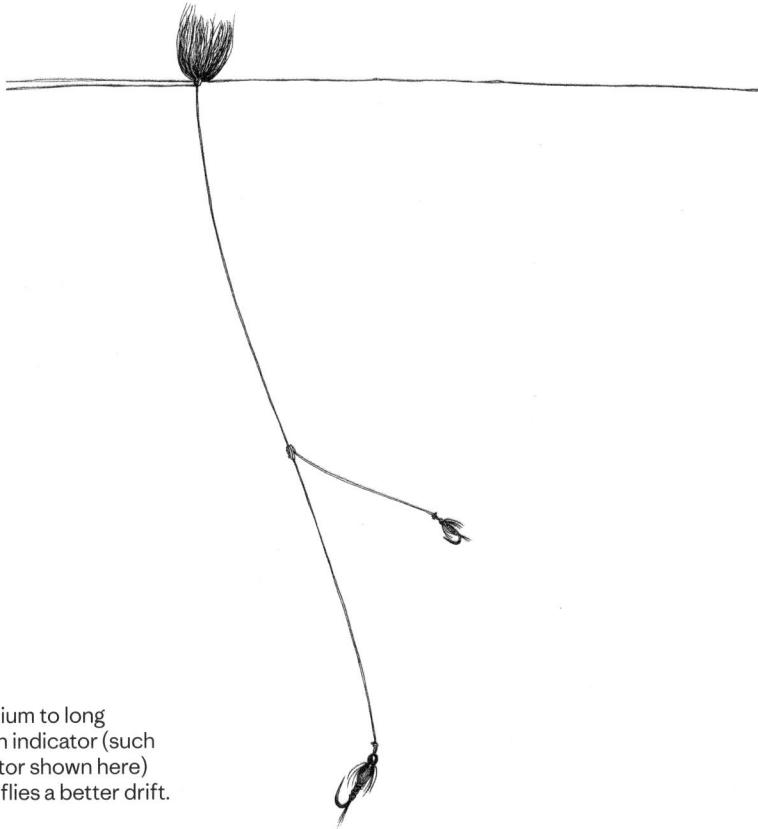

When fishing medium to long distances, using an indicator (such as the wool indicator shown here) will help give your flies a better drift.

Medium- and Long-Distance Nymphing

The longer the distance, the more difficult it becomes to get a natural drift, especially if you are trying to fish deep. An expert nympher will use various techniques to add slack to the cast: He or she mends the line to work the currents and employs subtle moves that are unteachable—and unknowable without putting in the 10,000 hours needed to truly master the craft.

The best we ordinary humans can do is resort to using a bobber or large dry fly as an indicator. The longer the distance, the more useful the bobber because it will enable you to keep more line out of the water, reducing the drag on your flies. If you're using two flies, extend the length between the dropper and the point fly to fifteen to twenty inches, which will allow you to cover a larger portion of the water column.

Casting overhead with two nymphs and a bobber will end in a mess if you try to make a standard dry-fly cast. Even worse, you could break the rod tip with the heavy bead flies. Instead, use an open-loop cast (Belgian cast) that keeps the flies and bobber apart from each other.

As soon as the flies touch the water, pull in the slack with your line hand; then follow the path of the flies, lifting the rod tip and retrieving line as necessary to maintain tension on the main line. The aim is to keep just enough tension to be able to feel the take and to set the hook, but not so much that it drags your flies. I believe it's better to err slightly on the side of more tension. I would rather allow a bit of drag than miss the fish that spits out the fly before I can react.

The fish may take at any point in the drift, but most often, the grab comes at the end when the line tightens, and the nymphs start rising to the surface in a perfect imitation of an emerging caddis or mayfly.

Mauro Mazzo at 2000 m in Valmalenco, Italy.
ALESSANDRO BELLUSCIO

The Belgian Cast

The Belgian cast is a constant motion cast, very useful when casting two or three flies at long distance, such as when fishing lakes.

*Watch
the video:
Belgian cast*

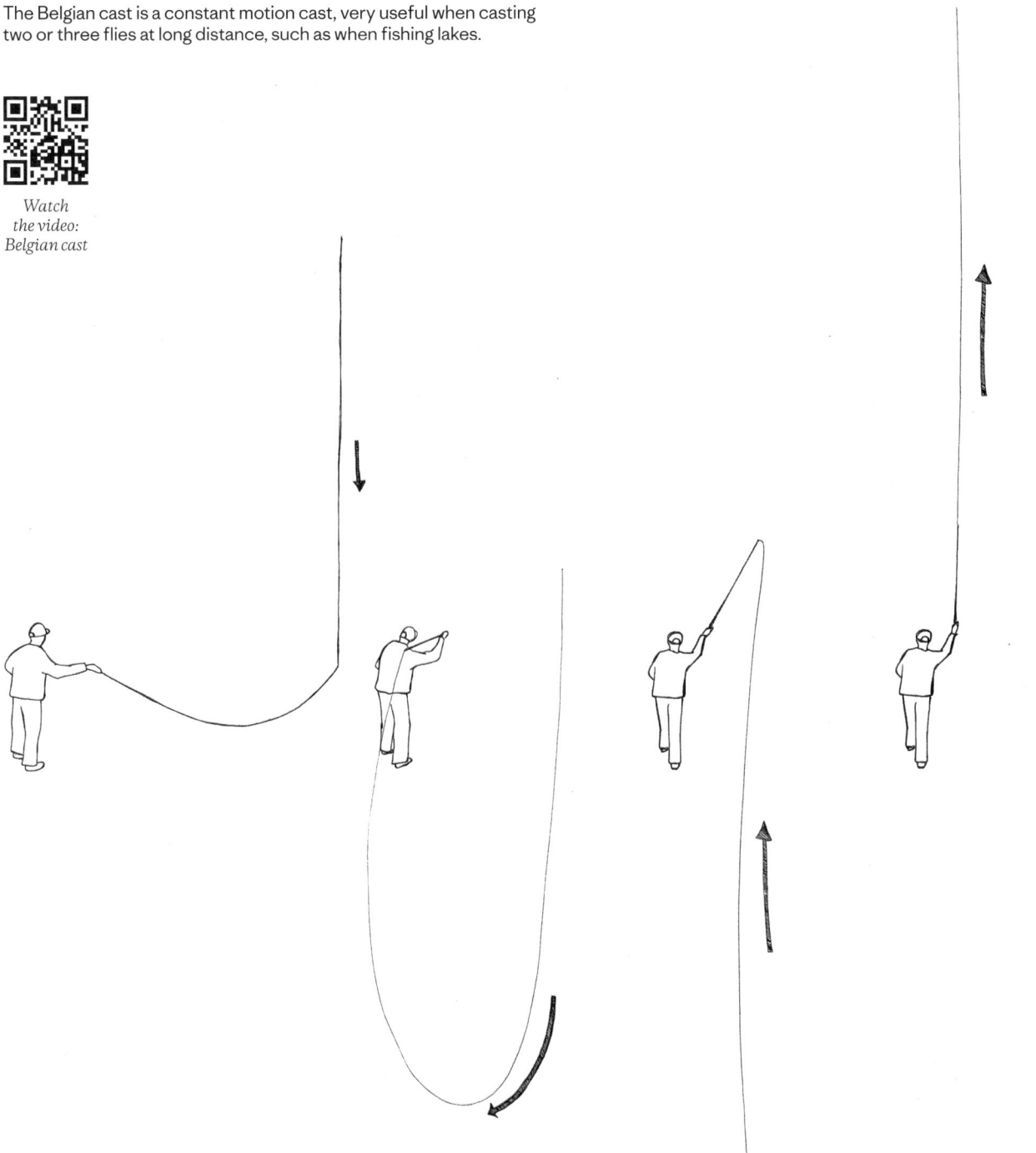

A

The cast starts by sweeping the rod back and to the side, almost horizontally. Note that the line is aerialized throughout the entire cast.

B

The rod maintains constant motion as it sweeps around the back, making an oval shape as it comes around and up.

C

The rod moves into a diagonal position as it begins to come forward.

D

The rod comes to a stop, and the line is released.

67

The Brake

When fishing in medium-fast to fast deeper water, the "brake" is a useful technique to keep your nymphs close to the bottom—where the fish usually are—for a longer time. This brake is the very essence of Euro nymphing. It is the key to having the nymphs drift at the same speed as the current they are in.

Cast upstream and give slack to the cast with an S, reach, or tuck cast so the nymph has a chance to sink before it is pulled by the line.

Remove any slack, then follow the path of your flies with your rod tip, as suggested in the previous section, until the line is nearly across from you and the leader is starting to drag the nymph at a speed faster than natural. Then put on the "brake" by lifting the tip and placing the line upstream. Doing so will reduce the line underwater and thus reduce the pull on the flies. If you are using an indicator or bobber, you can lift the whole rig and place it upstream. The most important thing is to not add any slack, which would cause you to lose contact with the fly.

Continue to mend or brake as necessary so the nymph is drifting naturally. Visualize the nymph sinking first and then moving up, imitating a nymph swimming to the surface. This motion often induces or triggers a fish to bite. This braking can be done several times during a drift depending on the depth and the speed of the water.

Watch the video: The brake

A Cast upstream, and after removing any slack, start the drift.

Underwater View

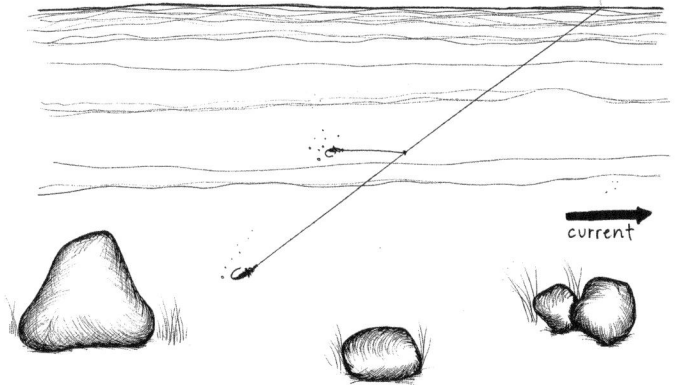

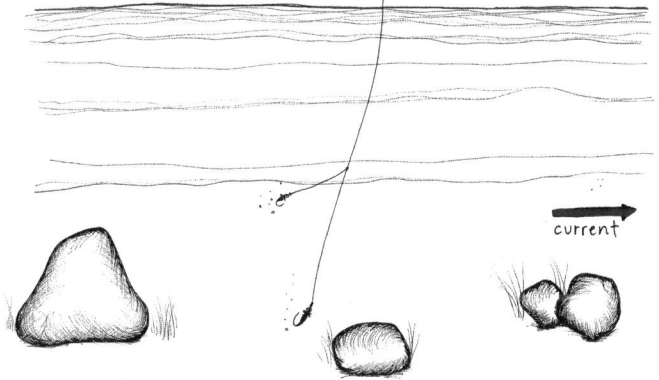

B   Once the line has moved downstream and has started to drag the nymphs, "brake" by lifting the rod tip and placing the line upstream. Do not add any slack. As shown in the underwater view, line drag causes the nymphs to drift faster than they would naturally and should be avoided.

Underwater View

C   Resume following the path of your flies with the rod tip, braking as necessary to maintain a natural drift. As shown in the underwater view, the desired drift will find your flies moving naturally in the current while remaining in contact with your line.

Pheasant Tail

Nymph Patterns

All nymph patterns listed may be used as a dropper or point fly, except for the Pheasant Tail Jig, which should always be used as a point fly. Each pattern may also be fished as a single fly.

Classic Pheasant Tail
Nymph

Pheasant Tail
Bead Head Nymph

Pheasant Tail
Jig

Pheasant Tail
Red Tag

Pheasant Tail
Caddis

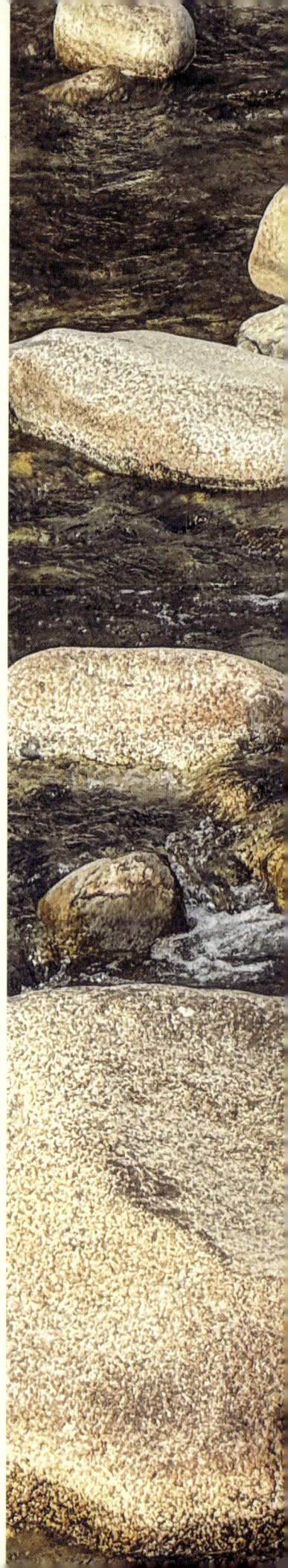

Mauro Mazzo nymphing with a short line. Keeping slack out of the line helps him detect subtle strikes. DANIELA PRESTIFILIPPO

Classic Pheasant Tail

Nymph

Frank Sawyer's Classic Pheasant Tail Nymph is both imitative and suggestive, and simple to tie. While Sawyer tied it to imitate the *Baetis* (also known as the Blue-Winged Olive) mayfly nymphs of England, much of the fly's success is because it is mistaken for many other species of mayflies. There is not a trout stream in the world with a species of mayfly whose nymph isn't matched by the Pheasant Tail. It should be the basic nymph choice for fishing any trout stream.

The pattern is fished blind before a hatch, or to specific rising fish during a hatch if fish are nymphing, and as an attractor during summer months.

It should be tied weighted using copper wire for a rib to fish near the bottom of the stream and unweighted without the rib to fish for trout feeding on nymphs in the surface film, or two to four inches beneath. Both versions are important to have in your fly arsenal.

MATERIALS

Hook: Umpqua UC600BL, #10–#20

Thread: 8/0 dark olive

Ribbing: Fine or extra-fine copper wire

Tail: 4-8 pheasant tail barbs (4 for #14)

Body: Pheasant tail barbs used for tail

Thorax: Hareline Hare'e Ice Dub, peacock

Wing case: Same barbs as used for the abdomen, or a strip of black Thin Skin plastic

Legs (optional): Four to six pheasant tail barbs

Watch the step-by-step video

73

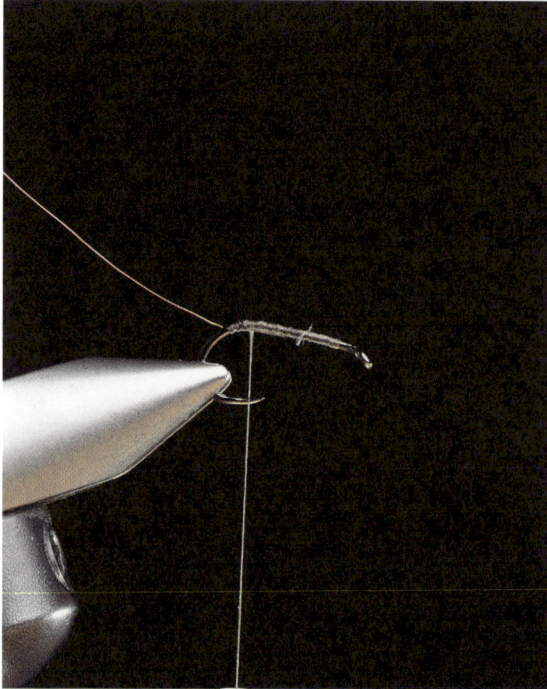

.01 Tie on the wire behind the eye. Wrap the thread to the bend of the hook.

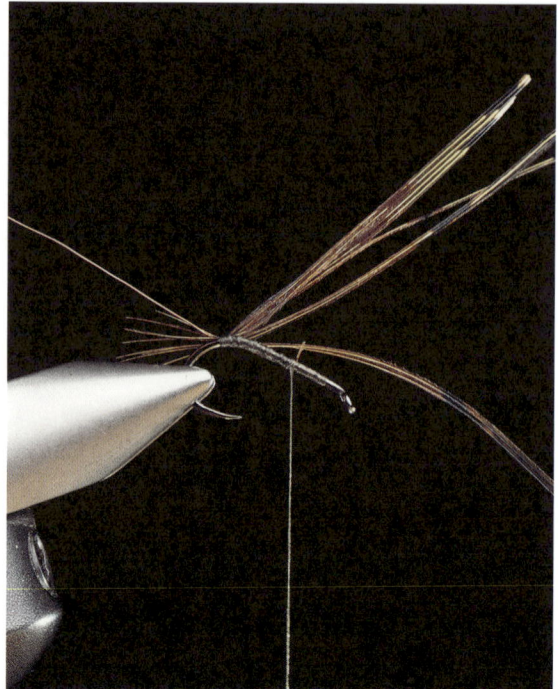

.02 Tie in four to eight pheasant tail barbs to form the tail, 1/8" to 1/4" long (1/4" for #14).

.03 Wind the barbs forward halfway up the hook to form the abdomen. Leave the barbs untrimmed, as they will become the wing case. If you wish to put on a plastic wing case, tie it in here.

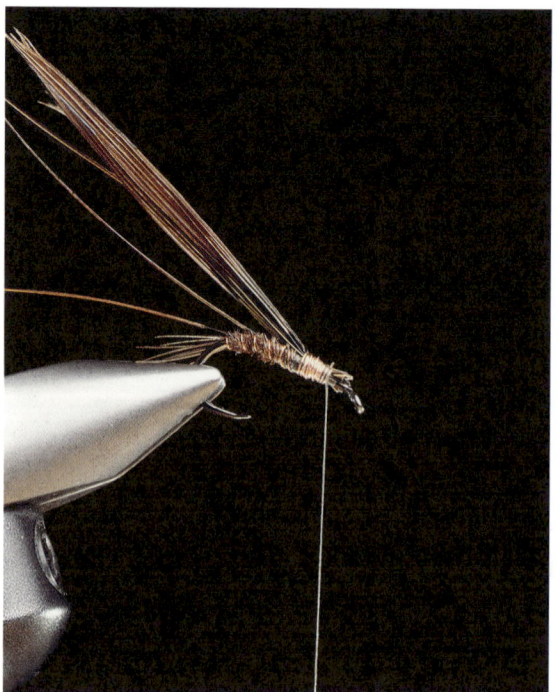

.04 Take four turns of wire to the front of the abdomen. You can add more weight by wrapping the wire several times at the thorax.

.05   Dub in the thorax.

.06   Pull the pheasant tail barbs or the Thin Skin forward over the top of the thorax to make the wing case. Using a bodkin, tease out the sides of the thorax to make short legs.

.07   Tie off and trim the excess and whip finish.

Pheasant Tail

Bead Head Nymph

This is an excellent deep-water nymph that can be used to imitate both caddis and mayflies. It differs from the Bead Head Flymph by use of the heavier tungsten bead.

MATERIALS

Hook: Umpqua UC610BL-BN, #10–#18

Bead: Black tungsten bead (7/64 inch for #12)

Thread: 8/0 Semperfli, olive

Ribbing: Extra-small to medium copper wire

Tail: 4-8 pheasant tail barbs (4 for #14)

Body: Pheasant tail barbs used for tail

Thorax: Hareline Hare'e Ice Dub, peacock

Hackle: Starling feathers

The steps to tie this fly are the same as for the Pheasant Tail Flymph and the Pheasant Tail Bead Head Flymph but with a heavier bead added at the beginning of Step 1. Reference the step-by-step recipe and the QR code to an instructional video for the Flymph on page 35.

After refusing every streamer, this brookie fell for a Pheasant Tail Bead Head Nymph.
BRYAN GREGSON

Pheasant Tail

Jig

MATERIALS

Hook: Umpqua XC400BL, #10–#16;
Umpqua UC655BL-BN, #10–#18

Bead: Copper

Thread: 6/0 UNI-Thread, black

Ribbing: Fine copper wire

Tag: Fine-to-medium red holographic tinsel

Tail: 6-10 coq de León grizzly hackle barbs

Body: 4-8 pheasant tail barbs

Thorax: Hareline Hare'e Ice Dub, peacock

Legs: Cul de canard feather, natural dun

*Watch the
step-by-step
video*

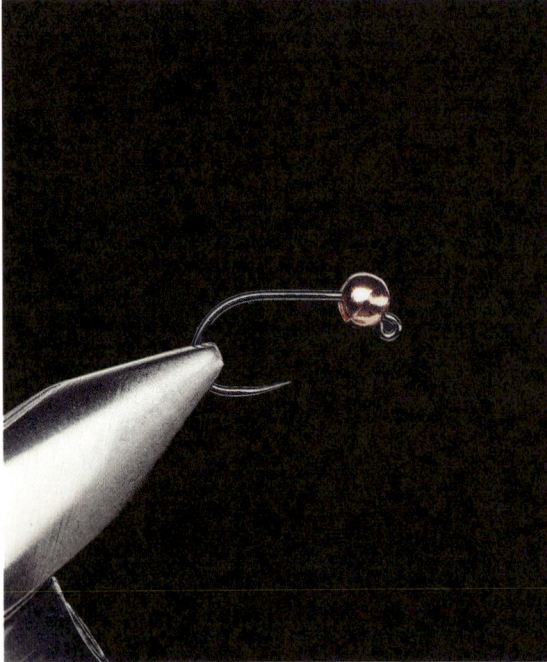

.01 Begin by sliding the copper bead head over the hook shank and forward to the eye of the hook.

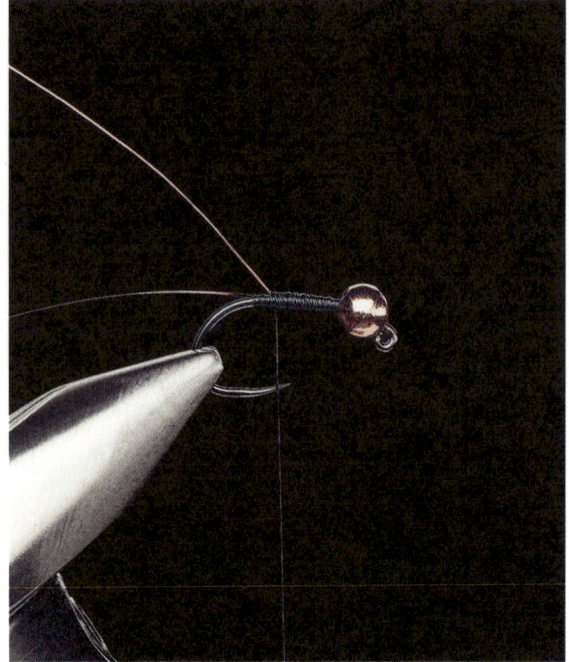

.02 Then wrap the thread and tie in the copper wire along with the fine-to-medium red holographic flat tinsel.

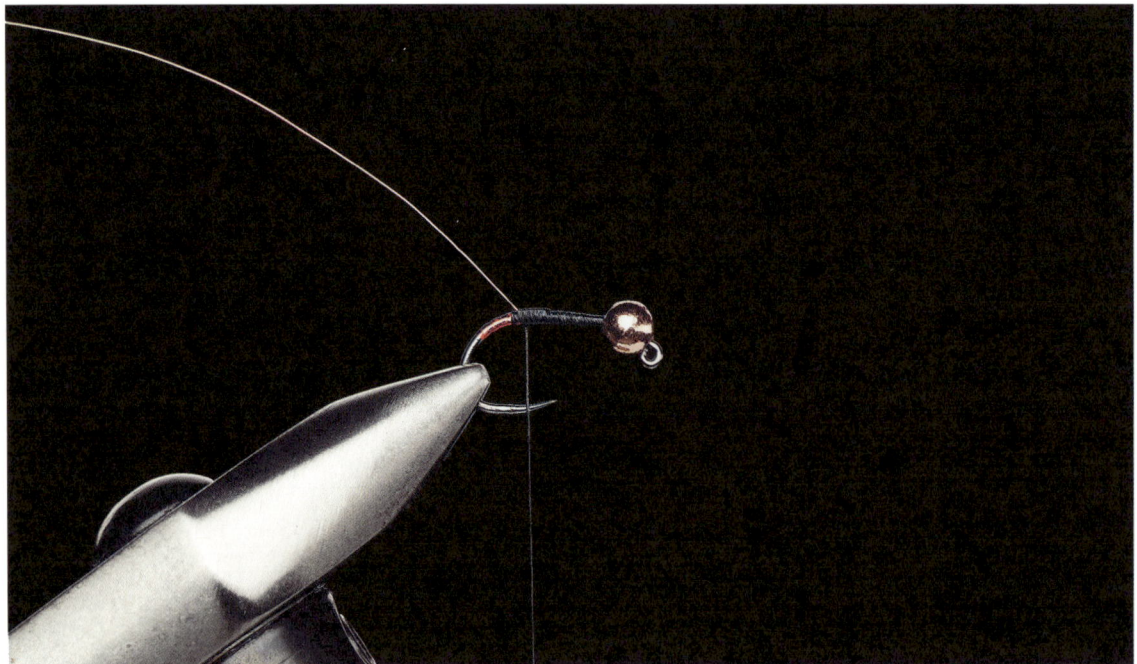

.03 Wrap several turns of the tinsel on the hook shank above the barb to make a short tag; then tie it off and trim it.

.04 Tie in six to ten coq de León barbs for the tail; then tie in four to eight pheasant tail barbs by the tips to make the abdomen.

.05 Next, wrap the pheasant tail barbs forward three-quarters of the way up the hook shank. Rib with four to five turns of the copper wire, and trim.

.06 Dub in the thorax with the Hare'e Ice Dub. Now, tie in a natural-dun cul de canard (CDC) feather and wrap one or two turns to make the legs. The legs should extend back to the bend of the hook. Tie off behind the bead and whip finish.

Pheasant Tail

Red Tag

MATERIALS

Hook: Umpqua UC610BL-BN, #14–#20

Bead: Copper

Thread: 6/0 UNI-Thread, black

Ribbing: Fine copper wire

Tail: Glo-Brite fluorescent floss, red, short

Body: Six to eight pheasant tail barbs

Thorax: Hareline Hare'e Ice Dub, peacock

Legs/hackle: Furnace rooster hackle

Watch the step-by-step video

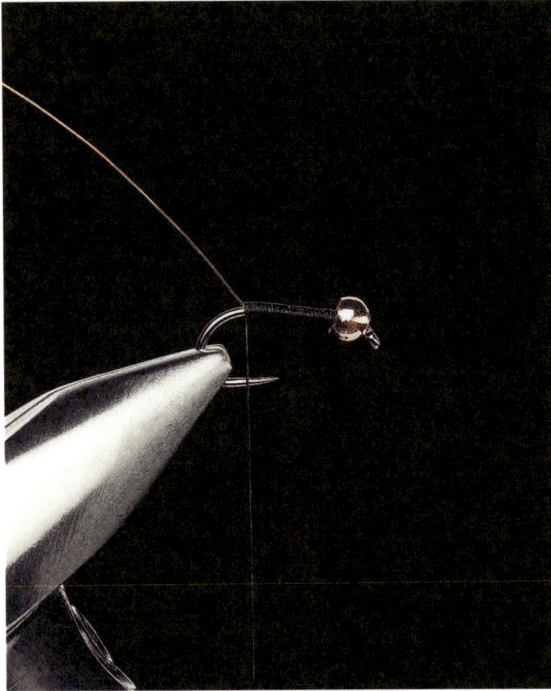

.01   Start by sliding a copper bead onto the eye of the hook. Tie on the wire.

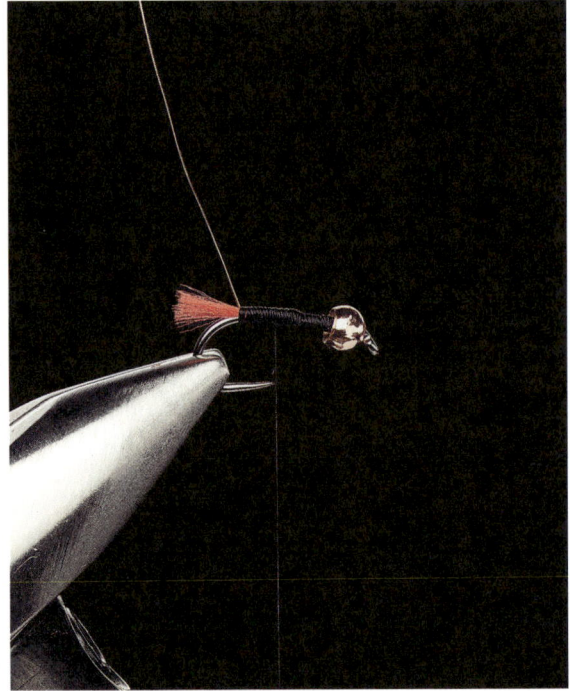

.02   Now, tie in a short piece of red floss for the tail. Trim the floss to about one-third the length of the hook shank.

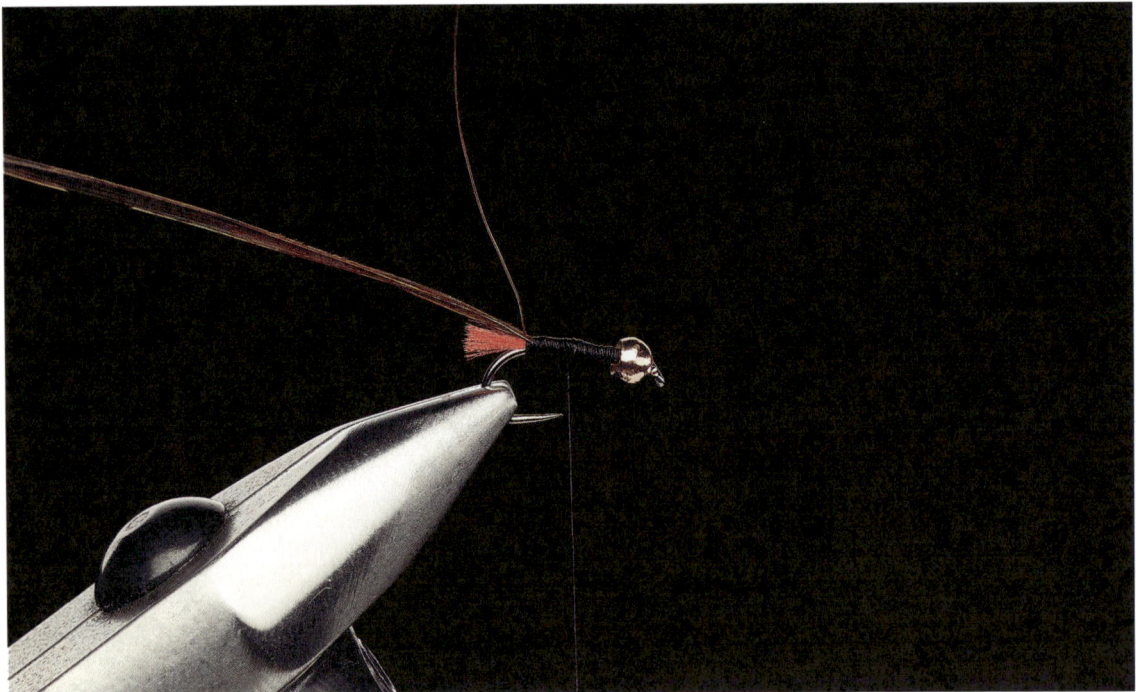

.03   Tie in six to eight pheasant tail barbs.

.04 Wrap the pheasant tail fibers forward to make a tapered abdomen, and rib with four to five turns of the copper wire.

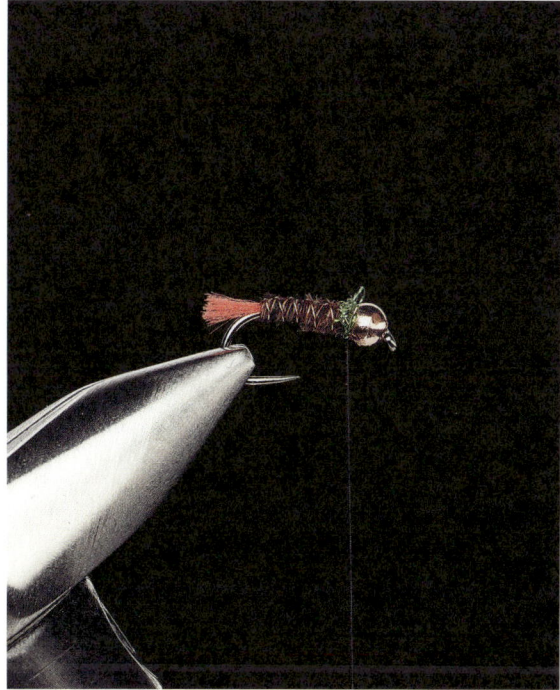

.05 Trim, then dub in the thorax with the Hare'e Ice Dub, leaving enough room behind the bead for the hackle.

.06 Now tie in the hackle and take two to three turns. Tie off behind the bead and whip finish.

Pheasant Tail

Caddis

MATERIALS

Hook: Tiemco TMC 2487BL, #12-#18; Umpqua UC625BL, #12-#18

Bead: Copper

Thread: 6/0 UNI-Thread, black

Ribbing: Fine copper wire

Tag: Glo-Brite fluorescent floss, orange

Body: 6-8 pheasant tail barbs

Thorax: Hareline Hare'e Ice Dub, olive brown

Watch the step-by-step video

.01 Begin the Pheasant Tail Caddis by slipping a copper bead over the hook shank. Wrap fluorescent orange floss down the shank and past the bend, then back to a point just behind the point of the hook.

.02 Tie off the fluorescent floss with thread, leaving a short tag exposed, and trim. Then, tie in the wire and six to eight pheasant tail barbs.

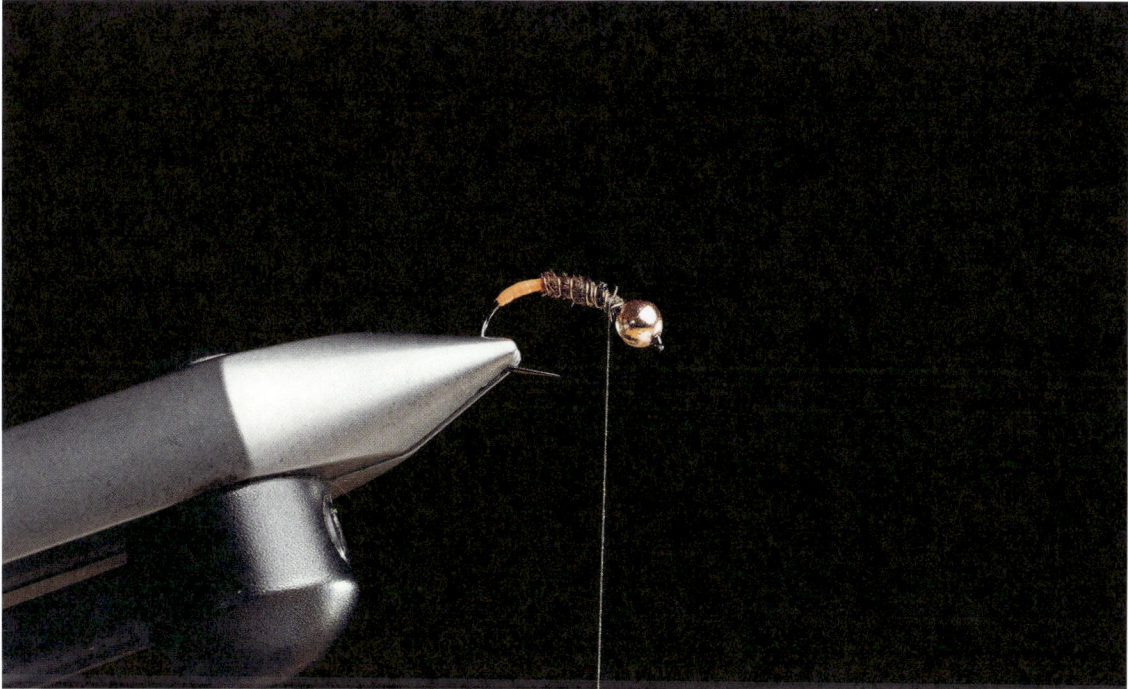

.03 Wrap the pheasant tail barbs forward toward the bead, leaving enough room to dub a short thorax. Rib the abdomen with the wire and trim.

.04 Finally, dub a thorax, finishing behind the bead. Whip finish.

Pheasant Tail Fibers, Simple Solutions to

Dry-Fly Puzzles

Craig Mathews

There were three big brown trout sipping emerging Pale Morning Dun (PMD) mayflies within six feet of my nose. I lay hidden from them in the grass along the shoreline of one of the premier spring creeks in the world, the same one Nick Lyons immortalized in his iconic book *Spring Creek*. These fish were no strangers to me; I had fished for them before, without success. In the past, I blamed it on my presentation. I thought perhaps drag might have been the issue, due to the creek's myriad microcurrents. Or maybe it was that smaller trout had taken my fly near the larger fish and put the big browns on alert. Even then they kept feeding, seemingly oblivious to me, to the smaller hooked and landed trout, or to my presentations.

This morning, though, I left my rod, reel, and fly vest behind in my truck parked more than two hundred yards downstream. I was determined to discover what those big, hook-jawed, male brown trout were really feeding on. I had tried No Hackles, Floating PMD Nymphs, standard PMD Sparkle Duns and Comparaduns, parachutes, cripple patterns, and other "guaranteed to work" flies with no success. I was rewarded with only a few small rainbows and browns rising in the lower part of the pool known as Fever Point. The three big fish I estimated at eighteen to twenty-three inches

Opposite: Brown drake. Silver Creek, Idaho. NICK PRICE

Above: Aha! The moment Craig Mathews discovers what the river says to do in order to fool big selectively feeding trout. RICH CROWDER

rose at the uppermost part of the big pool where the currents delivered the emerging duns to the waiting bruisers. In the past, I had observed these fish from well downstream, sitting on the bank and watching as they slowly finned up to inspect the emerging duns before deciding to sip one from the surface in a classic head-and-tail rise. I let them rise and take several naturals to establish their confidence, and only then did I present my fly on a short-line, pinpoint-accurate cast. I had done this on several occasions only to have the big trout come slowly to my fly, inspect it, and then turn its nose and drop to the bottom without taking my offering. It drove me crazy.

Today, I was determined to figure out if it was my presentation, my fly pattern, or both. I walked on my knees to within thirty feet, then lowered to my belly and pushed through the tangled buffalo grass and wheatgrass along the shoreline until I was nearly nose-to-nose with the three big trout. I could see their gill plates fanning as they filtered oxygen from the cold spring-creek water. I watched as a dozen fully emerged Pale Morning Duns with upright wings floated over the fish without a rise. At first, I thought my approach must have alerted them to my presence, but just then, the uppermost brown tipped upward and fed. I locked my sights on him; he was fewer than six feet away, slightly upstream and across from my position. As I waited for him to rise again, I observed several empty PMD nymphal shucks drift by. Then, he slowly rose again, and again.

Doing whatever it takes to get close to rising fish. This helps deliver a pinpoint-accurate cast that defeats drag while you keep track of the fly. RICH CROWDER

Large selectively feeding trout key on impaired emerging mayfly duns trapped in their nymphal shucks, recognizing them as easy meals. NICK PRICE

I thought, *Is he taking duns whose wings are stuck in their shucks? Or is he taking the impaired, crippled duns whose fully formed wings and legs or tails are still stuck in their nymphal shucks, unable to escape the surface film and fly off?* I watched him closely as he came to the surface and took another natural, then allowed a steady stream of fully emerged duns with upright wings to drift over him without rising.

I asked myself if he might be timing his rises, only coming up every few seconds, when he came up again, quickly followed by another rise. Then he allowed several fully formed duns to pass. He had now moved within a few feet of my position; he was so close I could see his near eye. Up to the surface he came again, and this time I saw what he took. I watched him rise several more times to make sure I knew what he was keying on, what brought those ultra-selective subtle rises of his to the PMD emerging duns. I smiled and said out loud to him and to his two big friends, now all rising together almost in unison, "You can no longer fool this guy, big boys, I saw what you're taking." The only insects they rose to were duns with partially trapped wings or legs still stuck in their nymphal shucks.

I continued to observe him and his partners for another half hour as they fed on the emerging duns before the hatch waned and the three big fish ended their feast and moved to the undercut bank nearby. It didn't take long for smaller trout to move in and begin recklessly feeding on the leftover mayflies. I drove home smiling, thinking of new fly designs that would solve the mystery lock these big fish had on me.

I had seldom considered color as a key ingredient in a dry-fly pattern for solving a selectivity problem like this one. But this day I had observed those three large brown trout taking only partially emerged, impaired duns. The main trigger I observed—the one that brought the fish to the crippled natural—was the color of the dun peeking out of its nymphal shuck as it struggled to escape and fly off the surface of the water. The three large brown trout recognized this behavior and keyed in on the impaired mayflies. Trapped in their shucks, unable to escape the surface, they were easy meals. Fish will not utilize more energy than is needed to feed on insects.

On my drive home to my fly-tying desk, I already knew the material I would use to imitate those partially emerged and impaired dun bodies: male ring-necked pheasant center tail fibers. These fibers imitate the natural brown and reddish-brown color of most of the important species of mayfly nymphs. This material can also be used to tie the stubby damp wings poking out from their two-tone bodies. I knew I could use the same material to design and tie similar patterns to imitate emerging caddisflies, midges, and stonefly bodies as well.

A heavy, wary brown trout fooled by a simple PT sparkle dun. RICH CROWDER

Pheasant Tail Fibers

I use the barb fibers from both sides of the two center tail feathers for my dry flies. Simply strip or clip off the desired barbs from the stem to create the proper taper and proportion of the natural insect being imitated. A general guide for dry-fly bodies is to use four barbs for hook sizes 8 to 12, three barbs for sizes 14 to 16, and one or two barbs for sizes 20 and smaller.

Pheasant Tail Dry Flies of the Past

I've been relatively surprised by the lack of dry-fly patterns designed with pheasant tail fibers. G. E. M. Skues, in his classic 1921 book *The Way of a Trout with a Fly*, mentions one pattern he designed using pheasant tail fibers to imitate the body of a "sherry-color, blue-winged olive mayfly spinner." Skues went on to say, after his design proved to successfully imitate the rusty-colored mayfly spinner, "I came to the conclusion that I had long neglected a very useful pattern, in the long hot evenings of July, August, and September, when the blue-winged olive is on, and the deep ruddy brown sherry spinner is plentiful."

Center tail feathers of a pheasant imitate the color and frilly nature of natural mayflies, caddisflies, midges, beetles, and other insects fish feed on.

I recall a conversation I had over thirty years ago with author and fly designer Datus Proper. He designed the Invisible-Hackle Fly to imitate a nymph that has moved to the surface in preparation to emerge but has not yet got its wings out of the nymphal shuck. Proper used two to three turns of light dun hackle in the design of this pattern, which he fashioned with pheasant tail barbs spun around waxed thread to represent the body of the nymph. This fly he designed "is an artificial nymph intended to sink."

More recently, talented Catskill fly tier and designer Seth Cavarretta of Bloomingburg, New York, published a short piece about his Pheasant Tail Dry Fly for fishing the Catskill waters. Using the center tail feathers to create the tails and abdomen of the pattern, he finishes with a thorax of peacock herl, wood duck wing, and furnace hackle.

The first time I used pheasant tail fibers in a dry-fly pattern, I was tying the bodies of October Caddis patterns to fish dry-fly steelhead on British Columbia's Morice, Bulkley, and Dean Rivers in the early 1980s. The idea wasn't mine; it came from Mike and Denise Maxwell, who designed their single and double Spey rods and fly patterns to fish steelhead on their home river, the Bulkley, out of Smithers, British Columbia.

Do-it-all dry flies, nymphs, and soft hackles for trout, salmon, and steelhead in fresh water, and for bonefish and permit in the salt.

Designing Simple and Effective Pheasant Tail Dry-Fly Patterns

In his wonderful little book *What the Trout Said*, Datus Proper relates that he knows many excellent fly tiers and anglers who simply cannot tie complicated fly patterns. I feel the same. These fine anglers and tiers tend to catch more fish than their peers. They will explain that they "absolutely see no need to tie difficult, time-consuming, and complicated flies." Simple, uncomplicated flies, tied with proper materials like pheasant tail, usually allow me to achieve my purpose for tying flies in the first place: to catch fish. Trout aren't impressed or influenced by complicated, artsy flies or by human emotions. They're impressed by simple, functional fly patterns that they recognize as the insects they are selectively feeding on.

Pheasant Tail Dry-Fly Equipment

I use either an eight-foot, six-inch, five-weight rod, or a nine-foot, three-weight for my dry-fly fishing. I prefer slow-action graphite rods that force me to slow down between presentations and concentrate on the float of the fly, rises of the fish, insects on the water, and the emergence stage the trout are rising to take. The slower-action rods also protect the fine tippets necessary to defeat drag and fool selectively feeding large trout.

I prefer a simple single-action, click-drag, lightweight reel that I've used for decades. My Hardy LRH Lightweight and Orvis C.F.O. Series reels continue to serve me well. Both give me a reliable drag system that protects the fine tippets and lightweight dry-fly hooks. They're strong enough to subdue even the largest wild rainbow and brown trout in the Madison, Henry's Fork, and Missouri Rivers.

Interestingly, few anglers know much about fly lines, yet they are the foundation of successful fly fishing. Most anglers are unaware that double-taper (DT) lines take up 30 percent more space on their reels than weight-forward (WF) lines. And most are also unaware that double-taper and weight-forward lines of the same weight have the same taper for the first thirty feet. Since most of my casting is within thirty feet, I prefer the weight-forward lines. Scientific Anglers Amplitude Smooth Trout Fly Line is a great example.

For large dry flies, size 8 to 16, I use Umpqua's nine-foot Perform X Nylon Leader, tapered from a butt diameter of 0.021 down to 4X, 7 pound (0.007 inch). The large butt diameter allows for smooth turnover of larger dry-fly patterns and pinpoint-accurate presentations. I use a double or triple surgeon's knot to tie a two- to three-foot section of 4X or 5X tippet to the end of the leader.

When fishing small dry-fly patterns sizes 18 to 28, I use a ten-foot Scientific Anglers Absolute Trout Stealth Finesse Leader, tapered from 0.18 down to 4X, 7.4 pound (0.007 inch). The small butt diameter of this leader provides delicate turnover and accurate presentation when fishing small dry flies. Then I use a double or triple surgeon's knot to tie two to four feet of a 5X, 6X, or 7X tippet to the end of the leader.

Lead has no place in a responsible angler's kit. Neither do barbed hooks. Because it takes a longer time to remove them, barbed hooks result in more time out of the water and greatly increase the mortality rate of the fish. You are going to release them anyway, so get rid of the cheat "ego" barbs. There are excellent competition barbless hooks available, but sometimes not in the smaller sizes from 20 to 28. In that case, find an alternative hook and pinch down the barbs before you tie them, so you don't forget to do it later.

Watch the video: How to fish a dry fly

Pheasant Tail

Dry-Fly Patterns

There are hundreds, if not thousands, of dry-fly patterns for imitating mayflies in their emerging, dun, and spinner stages.

Mayflies

Pheasant Tail
Mayfly Emerger

Pheasant Tail
Sparkle Dun

Pheasant Tail
Mayfly Spinner

Caddisflies

Pheasant Tail
Iris Caddis

Pheasant Tail
X Caddis

Midges

Pheasant Tail
Zelon Midge

Terrestrials

Pheasant Tail
Foam Beetle

C.M. in Yellowstone National Park.
There are big grizzlies and huge trout
on this small stream. JIM KLUG

Pheasant Tail

Mayfly Emerger

Emerging mayflies struggling to shed their nymphal shucks and become fully formed duns can be imitated easily and effectively by using pheasant tail fibers for their bodies.

When mayflies emerge, big trout usually feed exclusively on the impaired emerging mayfly duns that are stuck and trapped, trying to escape their nymphal shucks and become fully formed duns with fully developed upright wings. To imitate this situation, add a trailing, shimmering sparkling shuck to the pattern.

If selective trout tip up and inspect this pattern and turn away without taking it, I use a technique that has worked well on world-famous spring creeks and smooth-flowing rivers like the Missouri, Henry's Fork, and Yellowstone in Livingston, Montana. I present the fly two feet upstream of the rising fish, then gently pull it under the surface with a quick six-inch tug on the fly line. The fly will slowly gain the surface again, popping up right in front of the rising fish. This often results in an immediate rise to the emerger. Now simply raise the rod, letting go of the line as you do, or else you will break off fine tippets!

MATERIALS

Hook: Tiemco TMC 2488 Dry Fly and Nymph, #10–#24, or similar hook

Thread: 8/0 UNI-Thread or 12/0 Semperfli Classic to match thorax

Shuck (if desired): Zelon, mayfly brown

Abdomen: 4-6 pheasant tail barbs

Ribbing: Thread

Wing: Para Post, medium or dark dun, and/or cul de canard feathers

Thorax: Hareline Super Fine Dry Fly Dubbing or Semperfli Kapok Dry Fly Dubbing to match the natural coloration

Watch the step-by-step video

.01 Begin this simple pattern by tying in a shuck of mayfly brown Zelon, if desired.

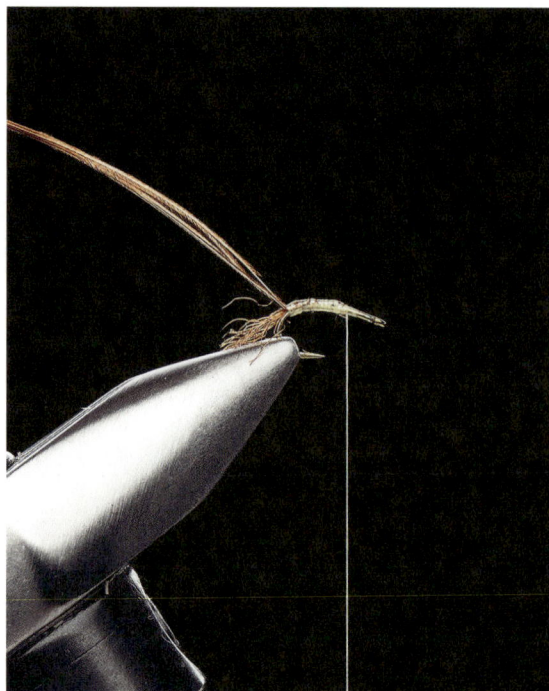

.02 Now, tie in four to six pheasant tail barbs.

.03 Wrap the pheasant tail barbs forward two-thirds of the way up the hook shank to form the abdomen. Reinforce the fibers and build the ribbing with an open criss-cross wrap of the thread, working to the hook bend and then back to the thorax.

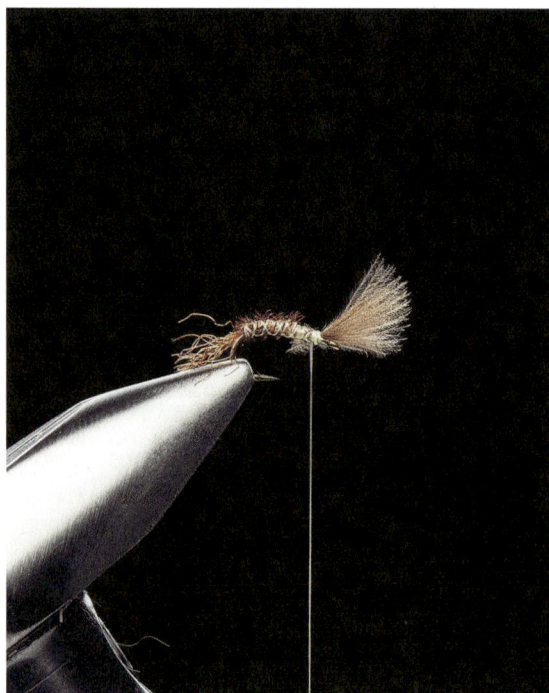

.04 Tie in a medium dun CDC feather, cocking the wing forward over the eye of the hook.

.05 Behind the CDC, complete the wing by tying in a clump of medium or dark dun Para Post.

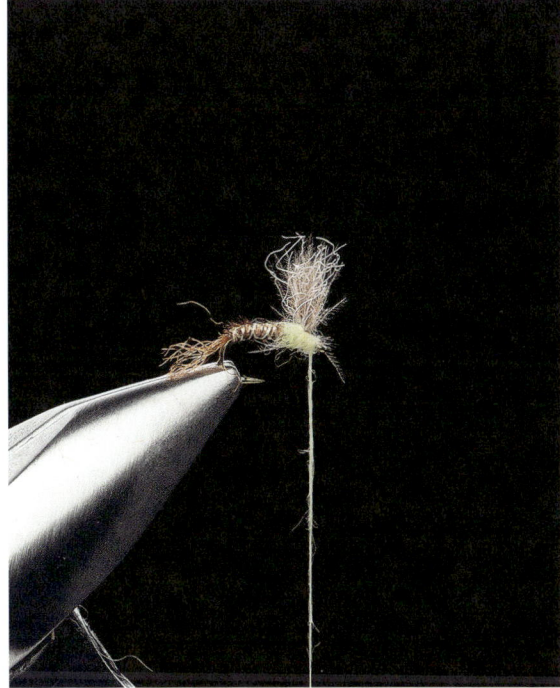

.06 Next, dub a thorax to match the coloration of the natural insect, then figure-eight the dubbing around the base of the wing, and dub forward to the eye of the hook.

.07 Whip finish.

A STORY

Impaired Duns

Several years ago, my fishing and former business partner, John Juracek, and I were fishing the selectively feeding rainbows on the Henry's Fork. We had used stillborn/impaired patterns first tied by Carl Richards and Doug Swisher and later written about in their classic book *Emergers*. We sat along the river at the famous Crossover Fence Pool to the Harriman Ranch, closely observing the big, wild rainbows sipping emerging Pale Morning Dun mayflies off the surface. It didn't take long to see the large trout keying in on the great number of impaired and stillborn duns coming down in the drift. Most of these duns were still attached to their nymphal shucks, which sparkled and shimmered in the morning light. The shucks were trailing the duns and still attached to the abdomen, trapping their tails, legs, or wings. Sitting on the bank observing those big fish taking these impaired and trapped duns, we knew what might have triggered the trout rising to the duns—the sparkling, shimmering, trailing nymphal shucks.

We sped the thirty miles back to our little fly shop to tie patterns to imitate the impaired duns. By combining a wing of deer hair for durability and floatability, a dubbed body, and a sparkling Zelon nymphal shuck, we created a dry-fly pattern that is easy to tie, floats like a cork, is visible, and produces better than any other no-hackle design or stillborn imitations we have tried. The sparkling shuck seems to be the key to this fly's effectiveness; it imitates the shuck better than any other pattern we have ever tried. The Sparkle Dun successfully imitates species of mayfly duns around the world, where it works its magic daily during mayfly emergences.

–C.M.

An impaired mayfly trapped in its shuck struggling to escape the surface is always easy prey for selective trout. ARVYDAS KIZEVICIUS / ALAMY

Selecting Proper Deer Hair

The key factors for picking out the right deer hair to tie Sparkle Duns and X Caddis are quite simple.

First, the hair must be *hollow*. Hollow hair easily flares, forming a perfect wing, and helps float the fly. The hollow hair butts also compress under the working thread, reducing bulk and enabling the fly to be properly proportioned.

Second, the hair should have the *shortest* black tips you can find. Black tips are found on all deer hair. The black tips are useless because they are fine and solid, resulting in a sparse wing that doesn't float, is harder to see on the water, and thus is not nearly as effective. It's probably worth saying again: Look for the shortest black tips for deer hair used in dry flies. This is especially critical when tying smaller-sized 18 to 24 Sparkle Duns.

And third, the hair should be *long enough to work with easily*. The hair used for tying tiny flies does not have to be short, just the tips do. Always look for hair that is long enough to grip comfortably.

Short, coarse, hollow deer hair with short black tips is perfect for winging Sparkle Duns.

Pheasant Tail

Sparkle Dun

When I see big trout feeding on fully developed mayfly duns with fully upright wings, I always fish a simple, easy to tie and to see, durable, and deadly Pheasant Tail Sparkle Dun.

Adding a shuck of sparkling Zelon material imitates the trailing, sparkling, and shimmering nymphal shuck still clinging to the legs, tail, or wings of the dun. Selectively feeding trout recognize the trailing shuck that prevents the insect from flying off, making it an easy meal. Large trout lock onto these impaired insects that are trapped in their shucks and unable to escape from the surface film. This makes the simple Sparkle Dun a deadly pattern to use during mayfly emergences.

The secret to tying this simple and easy pattern is using the correct deer hair for the wing.

MATERIALS

Hook: Tiemco TMC 100BL, #10–#24, or similar dry-fly hook

Thread: 8/0 UNI-Thread or 12/0 Semperfli to match the natural coloration

Wing: Natural deer hair

Shuck: Zelon, mayfly brown

Abdomen: 4-6 pheasant tail barbs

Ribbing: Thread

Thorax: Hareline Super Fine Dry Fly Dubbing or Semperfli Kapok Dry Fly Dubbing to match the natural coloration

Watch the step-by-step video

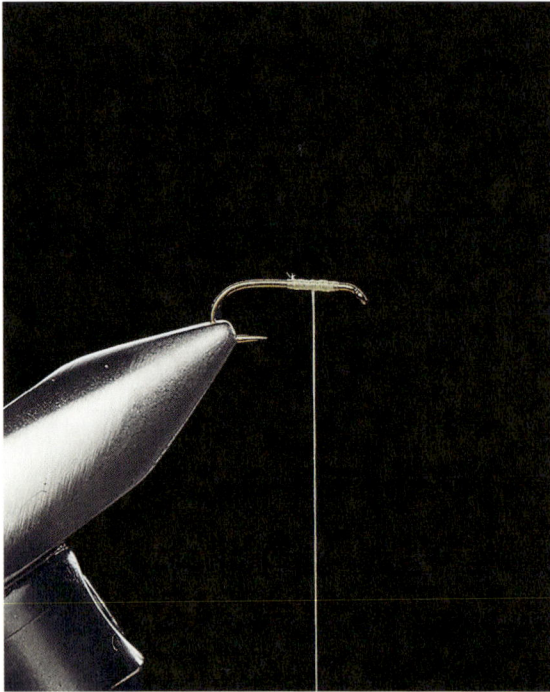

.01 Begin tying the Pheasant Tail Sparkle Dun by wrapping a foundation of working thread at the wing position.

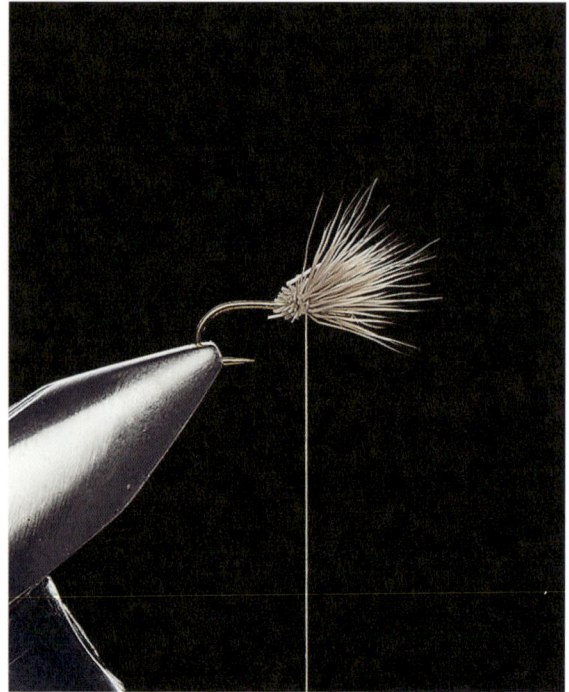

.02 Stack a clump of deer hair and tie it down with the tips facing forward over the eye of the hook. The wing should equal the length of the hook shank.

.03 Force one-half of the wing upright and take six to eight wraps in front of it; follow the same procedure for the remaining wing fibers. Good hair will flare on its own to create a 180-degree spread from one side of the hook to the other.

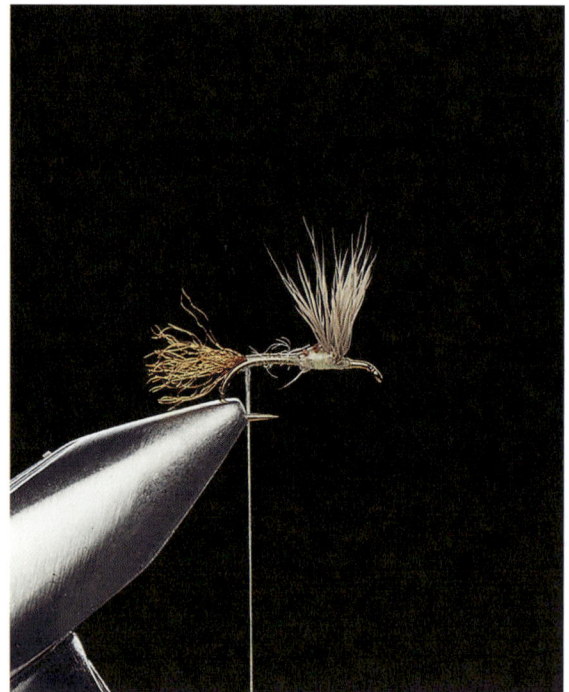

.04 Now, bring the thread behind the wing and tie in a shuck of Zelon that is just shorter than the hook shank.

.05 Tie in four to six pheasant tail barbs and wrap forward to the wing.

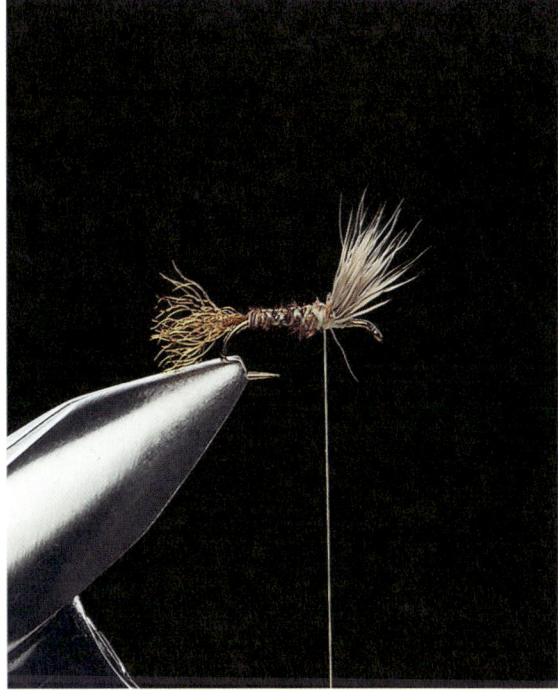

.06 Work the thread in crisscross wraps to the rear of the hook and back to the wing to reinforce the pheasant tail fibers and build the ribbing.

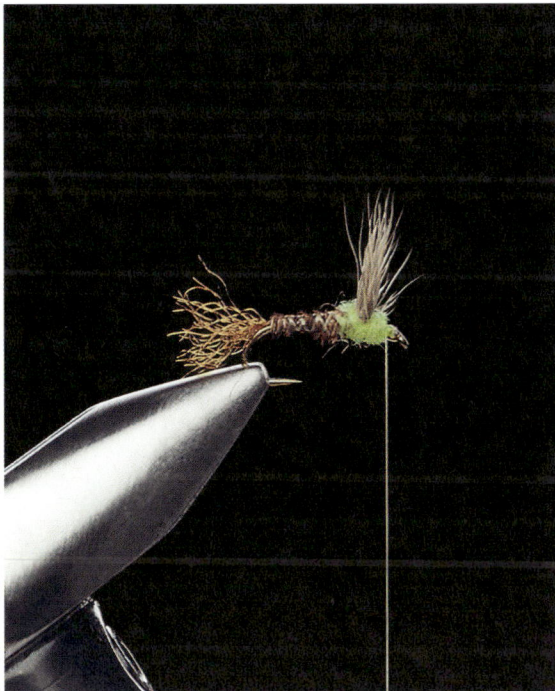

.07 Now, dub a thorax forward to the hook eye.

.08 Whip finish.

A STORY

Pale Morning Duns on the Firehole

Early last summer, I experienced two mornings of the finest and most productive spinner falls I have ever fished. The first morning was bright, warm, and sunny as I arrived at Wyoming's Firehole River to fish a Pale Morning Dun spinner fall. I knew it would be excellent since the day before I had fished a heavy hatch of duns on the river. The previous afternoon, prime weather conditions had brought heavy mayfly hatches. A cool, wet storm front had blown in, resulting in a couple of waves of mayflies.

I arrived at eight o'clock as the sun rose over the conifers and began heating the meadow stretch of the river. As I strung my rod, I noted several clouds of hundreds of PMD spinners hovering in the air above the river. The females were searching for males to mate with, and I knew I was in for some very good dry-fly fishing. It didn't take long for the first female spinners to fall to the river and release their egg masses. Within minutes, dozens of trout began to rise as I quickly knotted on a #16 Pheasant Tail Spinner to a fresh three-foot section of 6X tippet. I watched the smooth flows of the little river as bison grazed nearby. The trout took the naturals at the surface in a classic mayfly spinner rise indicated by slow porpoise rolls, showing their bodies, dorsal fins, and tails. I had the river to myself and took several fine rainbows and browns before the bison herd decided they wanted to cross the river where I was fishing, so I gave it up to them and headed to the Old Faithful Inn for brunch.

-C.M.

A magical river, the Firehole in Yellowstone National Park. Where else can one fish for rising trout as geysers erupt nearby? KEN TAKATA

Pheasant Tail

Mayfly Spinner

Fishing a mayfly spinner fall can be epic at times, but at other times, it can offer some of the most frustrating dry-fly fishing, even for the most seasoned angler. It is important to observe rise forms and do what the river is telling you to do.

The coloration of most mayfly spinners varies from rusty brown to olive and red and is imitated by the different shades of pheasant tail fibers. These same fibers can also be used to imitate the mayfly spinner's tails, abdomen, and wing case, making this fly a simple, effective, and easy one to tie.

MATERIALS

Hook: Tiemco TMC 100BL, or similar dry-fly hook, #16–#18

Thread: 8/0 UNI-Thread, rusty dun or red

Tails: 4-6 pheasant tail barbs

Abdomen: Same pheasant tail barbs as used for tails

Ribbing: Thread

Wing case: Leftover pheasant tail barbs from abdomen pulled shellback style over the thorax and tied off at the head to form a shellback

Wing: Grizzly or dun hackle barbs

Thorax: Hareline Super Fine Dry Fly Dubbing or Semperfli Dry Fly Dubbing, rusty spinner

Watch the step-by-step video

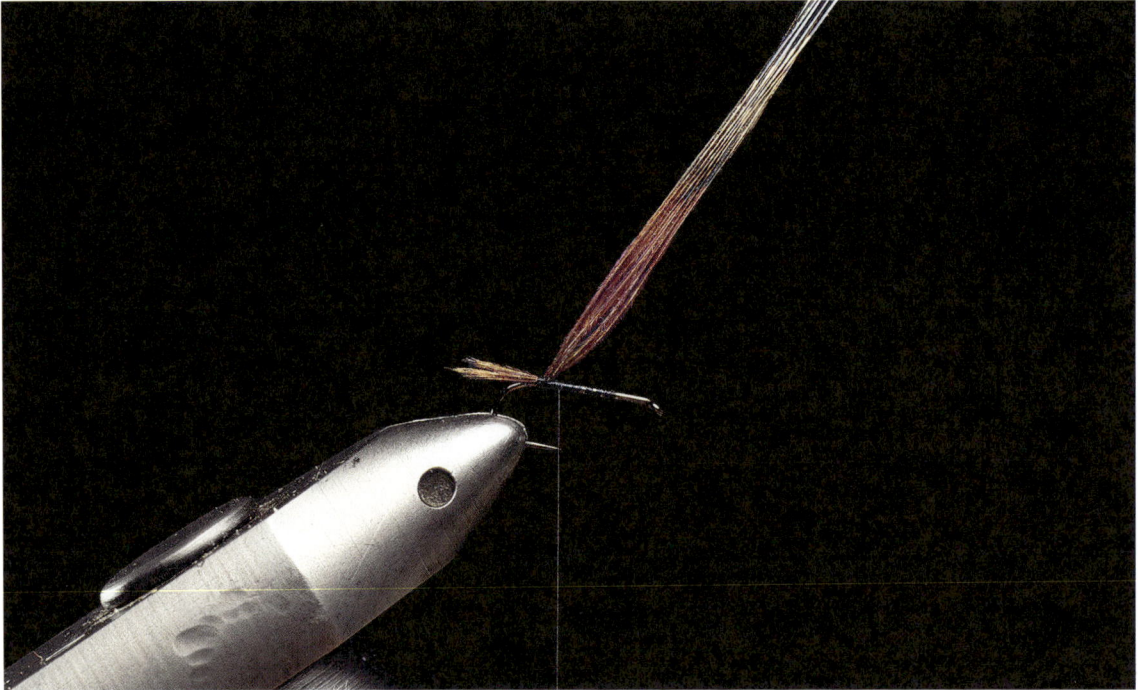

.01 Begin by stripping off four to six pheasant tail barbs and tying them in for the tails. Do not trim them; these barbs will form the fly's abdomen.

.02 Next, wrap the same barbs forward one-half of the way up the hook shank to form the abdomen. Again, do not trim them; allow them to stand up, as they will form the wing case. Work the thread in three to four open crisscross wraps to the tie-in point of the tails, and then return to the front of the abdomen to reinforce the pheasant tail fibers and build the ribbing.

.03 Tie in a light dun or grizzly hackle.

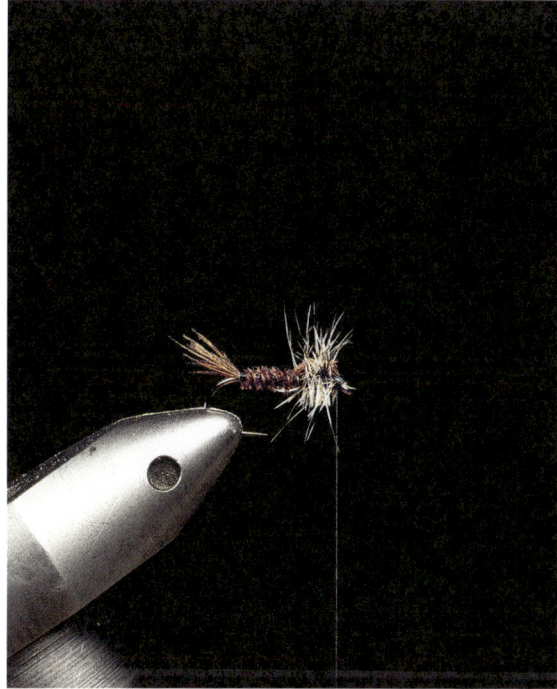

.04 Now, dub a thin thorax forward to just behind the hook eye. Wrap four to six turns of the hackle forward; then pull the pheasant tail barbs forward, dividing the top hackle barbs on either side.

.05 Whip finish and trim the hackle barbs flush with the underside of the fly.

A STORY

Recognizing Caddisfly Hatches

In his classic book *Caddisflies*, Gary LaFontaine notes three key signs of a caddis hatch. I expect to see them at my home river, Southwest Montana's Madison, nearly every evening in summer when caddis typically emerge. I arrive onstream just as the sun begins to set behind the Gravelly Mountain Range that lines the river.

When I leave my vehicle, I never string my rod. I walk to the river and find a pool, pocket, or run where I expect to find caddis emerging. I sit on the bank and enjoy the late-day scenery. As the light begins to fade, I see the first clue of a caddis emergence unfold before me. Small trout begin leaping in the air, chasing emerging caddis pupae. I tie on a fresh two-foot pull of tippet and select a Pheasant Tail Emerging Iris Caddis, knowing that if I remain seated and do not spray casts to the smaller trout rising in front of me, I will be in for some fine dry-fly fishing to larger trout.

The second, and perhaps strongest, clue to a caddis hatch is that no insects are visible on the water and yet fish are rising, a dead giveaway that caddis are emerging. Caddisflies are impossible to see on the surface of the water and seem to emerge and fly off unnoticed. It is important to remain still. I sit, waiting for the final clue indicating a strong caddis emergence. I know I won't have to wait long.

The third and final caddis clue comes with the failing light. The small trout that were aggressively rising cease coming to the surface. For several minutes, all rising stops, and just when I begin to think the larger trout won't rise this evening, I see bulging rises with dimples, porpoise rolls, and even tails breaking the surface. These now become the more common rise forms. I will pick my target and begin to fish to the larger trout that have taken over the pools, pockets, and runs of the river.

–C.M.

Important clues for fishing caddis emergences.
JESSICA MCGLOTHLIN

Caddisflies are the insects least understood by anglers, but they are as significant as mayflies to dry-fly anglers. There are an amazing number of dry-fly patterns intended to imitate these insects, and these patterns are often confusing. Designing simple and effective caddisfly patterns has presented challenges to fly tiers over the years. But the pheasant tail flies listed here will solve the puzzles and challenges inherent in fooling even the most selective trout. These patterns will work their magic no matter what stage of dry-fly caddis activity—from emerging to egg-laying to spent adults—the big fish are feeding on.

It is largely caddis emergences that frustrate most anglers. Being able to recognize when caddisflies are hatching is the first step in understanding them.

Here are the techniques I use and pheasant tail dry flies I present to fool those larger fish until as late as eleven o'clock nearly every summer evening.

Watch the video: Caddisfly techniques

Subtle, porpoise-like rise-forms from big trout rising to emerging caddis. Snake River, Idaho. JEREMIAH WATT

Pheasant Tail

Iris Caddis

Because most caddis emerge and leave the water quickly, many fly designers believe that trout might favor an impaired or stillborn insect that they've learned over time is going nowhere, because its body and wings are trapped in its pupal shuck. In our little book *Fly Patterns of Yellowstone*, volume 2, John Juracek and I wrote about designing an emerging caddis imitation that would float well and be visible, especially during late evening's failing light when most caddis hatch and fish feed on them. We had collected samples of emerging caddis and tried several materials to imitate those sample specimens. We ended up imitating the shuck and partially emerged wings with sparkly, shimmering Zelon yarn. Over time, I've used pheasant tail more than standard dubbings to imitate the body. The frilly nature of the pheasant tail barbs traps air bubbles and naturally sparkles, closely imitating an emerging caddis. The pattern floats high, and the visibility of the wing helps make it easier to keep track of in late-evening light. We call our pattern the Iris Caddis. In larger sizes, the fly can be used effectively as an attractor fly because it floats well and is easy to see; it imitates foods that trout recognize and are used to feeding on. This simple fly is the most effective of all emerging caddis dry-fly patterns we have ever fished.

A technique I often use if fish refuse to take a dead-drifted Iris is to skate or skitter it in front of a working fish. Usually this results in an aggressive take, so be prepared to raise your rod and let go of the fly line, or you will break off big fish.

MATERIALS

Hook: Tiemco TMC 102Y, or similar dry-fly hook, #15–#19

Thread: 8/0 UNI-Thread, rusty dun

Shuck: Zelon, caddis color, half the length of the body

Body: 4-6 pheasant tail barbs

Ribbing: Thread

Wing: Zelon, cream or dun

Thorax: Hareline Hare's Ear Dub

Watch the step-by-step video

.01   Tie this effective pattern by first attaching a piece of Zelon at the rear of the hook to imitate the shuck.

.02   Now, tie in four to six pheasant tail barbs to form the abdomen and wrap them forward two-thirds of the way up the hook shank.

.03   With four to five open crisscross wraps, return to the bend of the hook and back to the top of the abdomen.

.04 Next, pinch a strand of Zelon between your thumb and forefinger and fold the ends to make a loop. This loop forms the wing and gives it dimension, and the strands will fluff up, giving the wing some height and making it more visible. Tie it tightly on top of the hook. Do not trim it; leave the butt ends facing forward over the eye of the hook.

.05 Dub a head of Hare's Ear in a figure-eight pattern around the wing butts; then trim them, leaving the ends peeking out of the head to aid in floatation and visibility.

Pheasant Tail

X Caddis

The Pheasant Tail X Caddis is arguably the simplest dry caddis pattern on the planet. The reason for the design of this important fly was simple: If big selective trout took Sparkle Duns with trailing shucks that imitate emerging and impaired mayflies, why wouldn't the same thing work for caddis imitations? Caddis, like mayflies, can experience difficulties escaping their pupal shucks. Many end up trapped with their shucks trailing off their wings, bodies, or legs. Big, selective trout will usually refuse to take high-floating patterns like Elk Hair Caddis, instead feeding on simple impaired adults like the X Caddis. Using pheasant tail fibers for the body of the adults with a trailing shuck of Zelon and deer- or elk-hair wings is a deadly combination. Simple, durable, easy to keep afloat, and visible, this fly perfectly imitates the low profile and silhouette of adult caddisflies trapped in their pupal shucks.

Don't be afraid to give the X Caddis some movement should fish refuse to take your dead-drifted imitation. I like to pull my pattern under the surface and allow it to pop back up to the surface right on the nose of fish feeding on the emerging caddis. This technique usually results in an immediate rise to the fly.

MATERIALS

Hook: Tiemco TMC 100BL or similar hook, #14–#20

Thread: 8/0 UNI-Thread to match body color

Shuck: Zelon, caddis color

Body: 4-8 pheasant tail barbs

Ribbing: Thread

Thorax: Olive, amber, or tan Zelon Dubbing Blend

Wing: Deer hair

Head: Trimmed butts of deer-hair wing

Watch the step-by-step video

.01   Begin the Pheasant Tail X Caddis by tying in a shuck of Zelon, extending it to just short of the length of the hook.

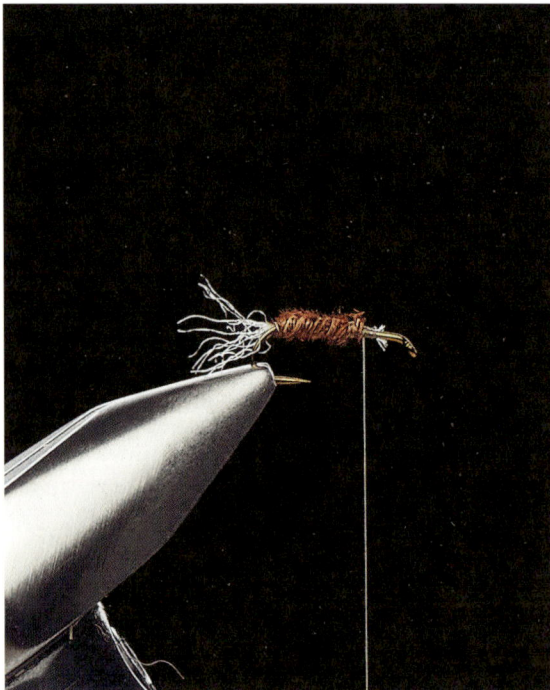

.02   Next, to form the abdomen, tie in four to eight pheasant tail barbs and wrap them halfway up the hook shank.

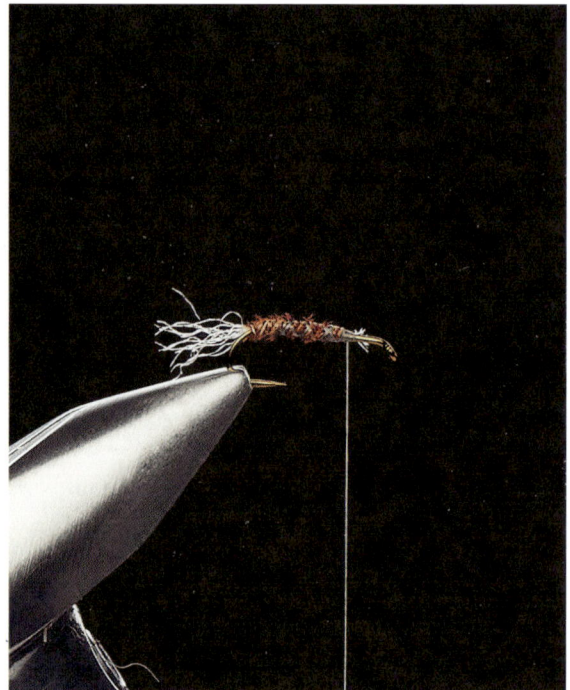

.03   Tie them off, then work the thread in crisscross wraps to the rear of the hook and back to the tie-off point to reinforce the pheasant tail fibers and build the ribbing.

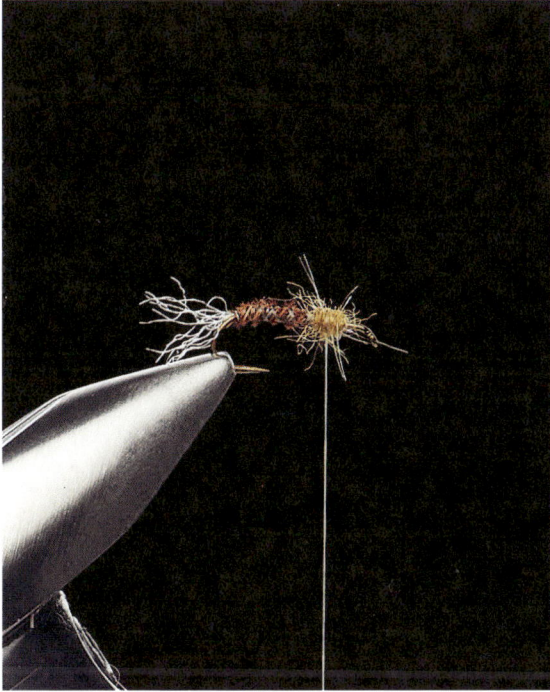

.04   Dub in the Zelon blend, leaving enough room to tie in the deer-hair wing.

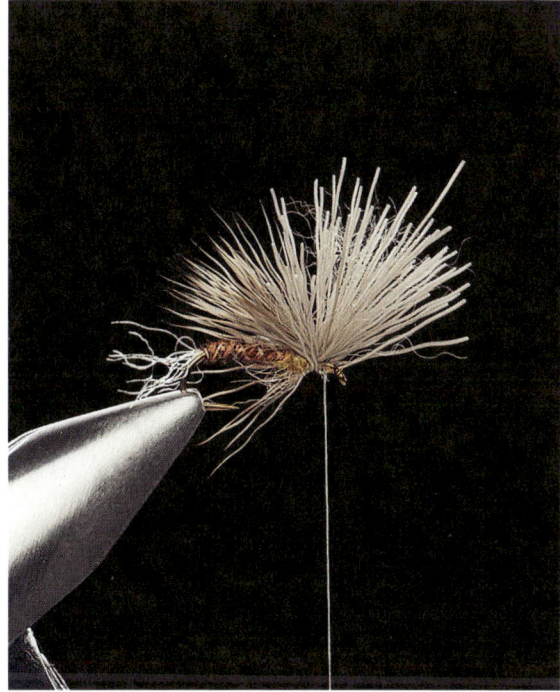

.05   Now, stack a deer-hair wing and tie it on, extending it to the hook bend. The wing should be full and cup the body, extending down over the sides of the fly.

.06   Whip finish and trim the wing butts.

A STORY

Self-Respecting Trout

It was over thirty years ago on the Madison River near the Raynolds Pass Bridge. It was calm and clear, and the temperature struggled to reach twenty degrees that December day. Bored with the lack of interest from any trout or whitefish, I continued chucking a heavily weighted #4 black rubberleg stonefly nymph behind a boulder, mindlessly watching my strike indicator as it bobbed along in the current, hoping it would hesitate or jerk forward indicating a fish's take. My attention was drawn to a pair of mature mallards as they lifted off the quiet water near the shoreline. I wished I'd had my shotgun, since I'd promised friends duck for Christmas dinner.

Standing there watching the ducks circle back around, I caught a flash of light coming off the quiet water near where the ducks took off. I focused on the spot and could see fish rising. I muttered, "No self-respecting trout is gonna rise in twenty-degree temps. What the heck would they rise to in freezing temps like this, anyway?" I reeled in and put my near-frozen hands in my pockets. I watched the water for more rises and tried to spot what they were coming to the surface to feed on. Closely focusing on the surface, I could see tiny two-winged flies, midges, hovering an inch or two above the water in the microclimate that allowed them to do so even with air temperatures ten degrees below freezing. As I watched those rising fish that day, I decided it was time to tie some midge dry flies and learn to fish them. I soon discovered that at no other period during the fishing year could I see more fish rising to insects than in the cold of winter. Trout relish midges and rise to them all year long, creating the finest dry-fly fishing opportunities for those willing to fish small flies on light tippets.

–C.M.

Craig Mathews fishing southwest Montana.
FORREST MANKINS

Pheasant Tail
Zelon Midge

For many years I avoided fishing tiny midge dry-fly patterns, until I realized I was missing some of the best dry-fly fishing opportunities of the year. I remember the first time I tried midge fishing.

Midges emerge nearly every day of the year on trout waters around the world and are important to trout and anglers. Trout feeding on emerging midges can be the most difficult fish to fool, so many anglers stay away from tying tiny midge patterns and fishing midge times. That's unfortunate, since a simple, easy-to-tie, dry midge fly can fool big trout feeding selectively on emerging adults. When fishing a dry fly to a rainbow feeding on winter midges or to a wily New Zealand brown, it's best to make your first cast with a small fly. It's less likely to put the fish down if you blow the cast or have drag on the fly. Many anglers are surprised to learn we have excellent midge fishing on big western rivers. Midges are also important to both fish and anglers on spring creeks and lakes.

The Pheasant Tail Zelon Midge is an imitation of an emerging midge trapped in its pupal shuck. Trout feed eagerly on trapped emergers since they recognize these crippled, helpless insects are unable to leave the surface of the water. During heavy midge hatches when big fish are taking drifting midge pupae, this fly will work better than a standard pupal pattern.

The pattern floats well when treated with floatant and dusted with desiccant powder that makes the Zelon wings very visible. It is worth noting that the best approach to fish that are rising to midges is usually across and downstream to enable a drag-free presentation on light 6X to 7X tippets. On rivers with pools and pockets, like the Madison, a straight upstream approach is best. It is important to get as close to rising fish as possible to allow for a short pinpoint-accurate cast to defeat drag and detect the fish's rise to the fly. When the trout does take the fly, slowly raise the rod; fish are in no hurry when feeding on midges, so be patient and allow the trout to completely inhale your tiny fly.

MATERIALS

Hook: Tiemco TMC 2488 or 100BL, or similar hook, #18–#26

Thread: 8/0 UNI-Thread to match body color
(olive dun or black is the most common)

Shuck: Zelon or Para Post, medium or dark dun, or none

Body: The shuck, ribbed

Wings: Zelon or Para Post, medium or dark dun

Thorax: 2-3 black natural pheasant tail barbs

Watch the step-by-step video

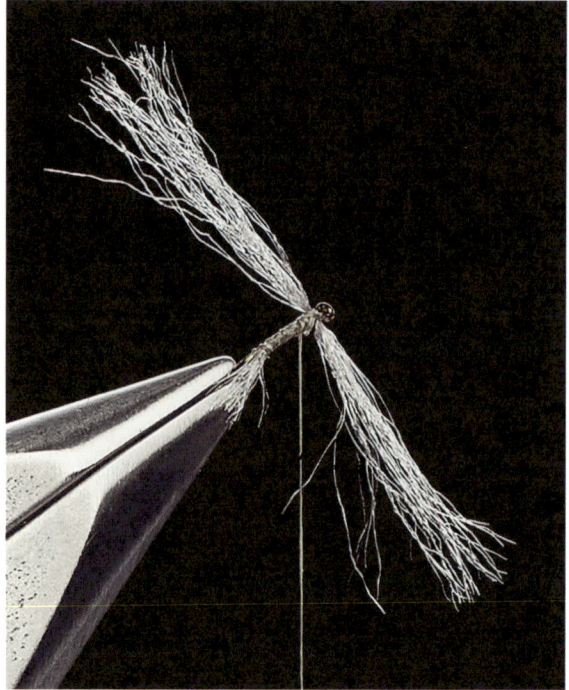

.01 Begin by splitting a strand of Zelon in half, tying it in for both a trailing shuck and the abdomen. Wrap the thread up the shank of the hook, ribbing the Zelon half the length of the shank to form the thin abdomen.

.02 Next, tie in a Zelon wing with figure-eight wraps around the base of the wing so they stand out perpendicular to the hook shank.

.03 If desired, sweep and hold the wings back forty-five degrees with wraps of thread, or leave them standing out at ninety degrees—the fish won't care either way.

.04 Now, strip off two to three pheasant tail barbs and figure-eight-wrap them around the wings.

.05 Whip finish.

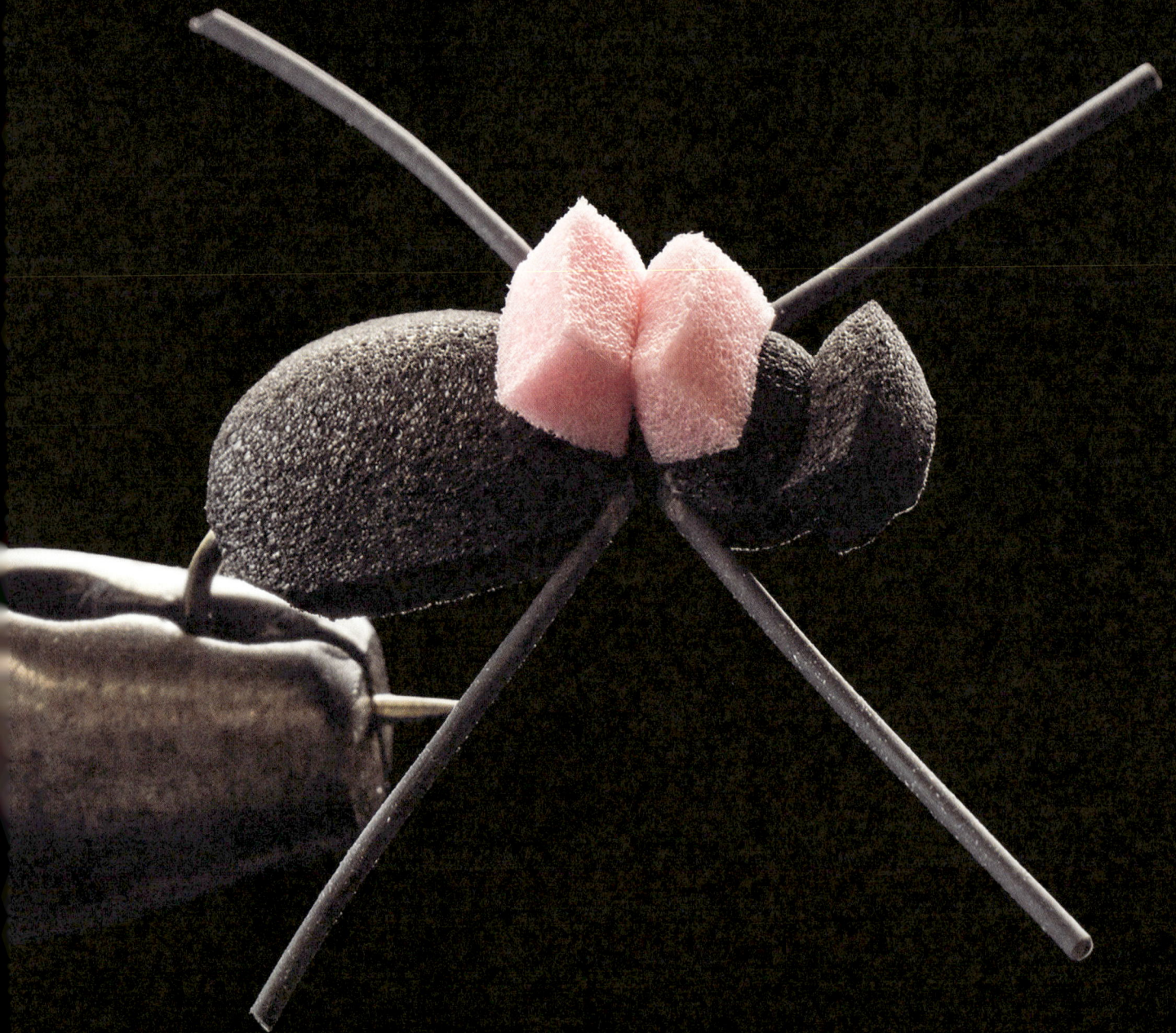

Pheasant Tail

Foam Beetle

Among fly designers and fly tiers, and many veteran anglers, the argument that big cutthroat trout are attracted to big floating foam flies continues. Nick Nicklas, one of the most innovative and talented fly designers, sadly passed away in 2014, but his flies live on through the wonderful fly designs he left anglers. His Crystal Beetle is one of those patterns.

Nick felt he could capitalize on the cutthroats' interest in huge floating flies by luring them into taking an oversized version of something like a beetle, a known and recognized food item.

The Pheasant Tail Beetle, a variation of Nick's Crystal Beetle, substitutes a body of pheasant tail fibers for the Crystal Chenille he used in his design. I have found that rainbow and brown trout might shy away from the shine of the Crystal Chenille, so I began tying bodies made of pheasant tail fibers, with good success. One thing big trout can be counted on to investigate is the *plop* a natural or imitation insect makes while clumsily falling into the water. Beetles, especially large ones, bumble along the shoreline and often tumble into the water. Some species like the longhorn beetle crash and burn as they fly over the water and mistake it as a place for a solid landing. In any case, the big trout's take is often heard rather than seen when the fish noisily slurps in the Pheasant Tail Beetle.

I have taken trout on the Pheasant Tail Beetle every month of the year. In winter, before or after midges bring trout to the surface—usually from noon to three o'clock—I can blind cast this fly and bring trout to it.

MATERIALS

Hook: Tiemco TMC 100BL, or similar dry-fly hook, #8–#16

Thread: 6/0 or 8/0 UNI-Thread, black

Shellback: Black closed-cell foam, 2 mm

Body: 6-10 pheasant tail barbs

Legs: Fine rubber legs

Indicator: Brightly colored closed-cell foam, usually orange or pink

Head: Trimmed butt of shellback foam

Watch the step-by-step video

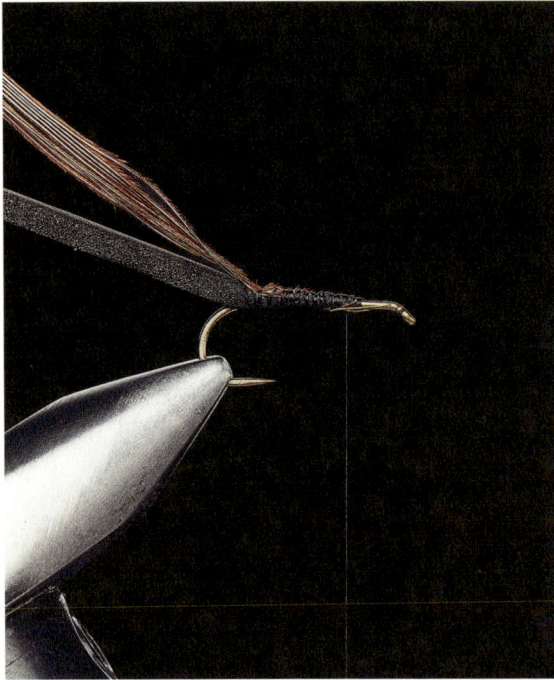

.01   Tie in a strip of black closed-cell foam atop the hook, followed by six to ten pheasant tail fibers above the hook bend to form the body.

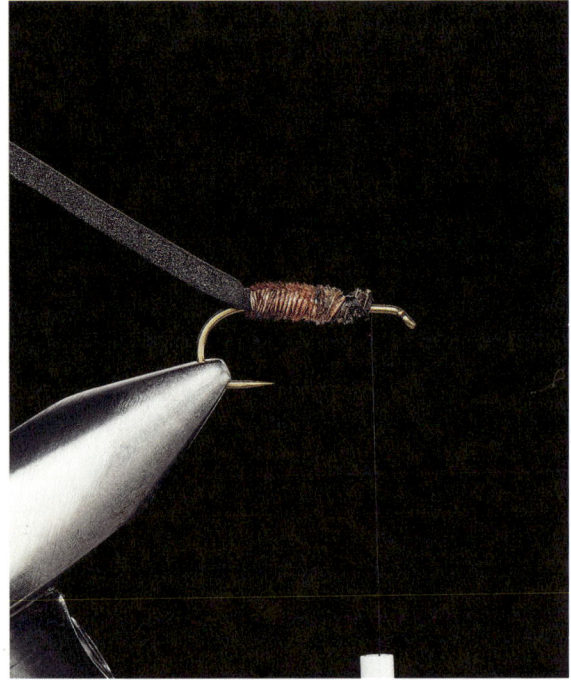

.02   Next, twist the barbs around the working thread and wrap them forward, leaving enough room to tie in the shellback foam.

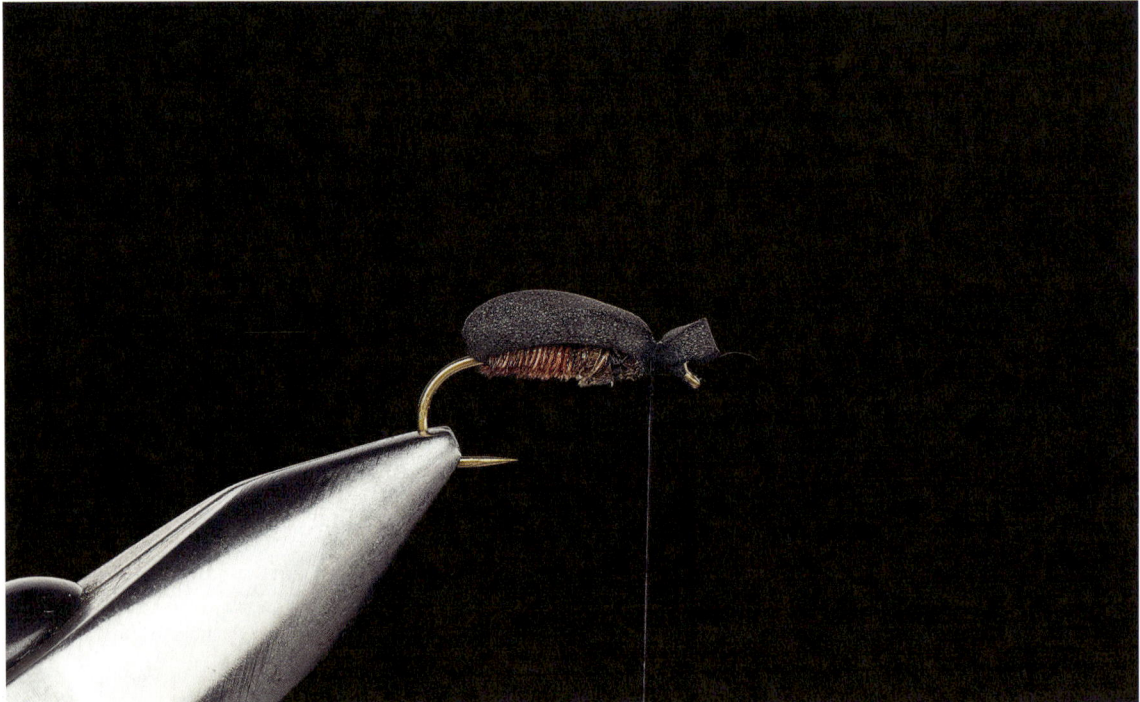

.03   Now, fold the foam strip over the top of the body and secure it with thread wraps behind the eye of the hook.

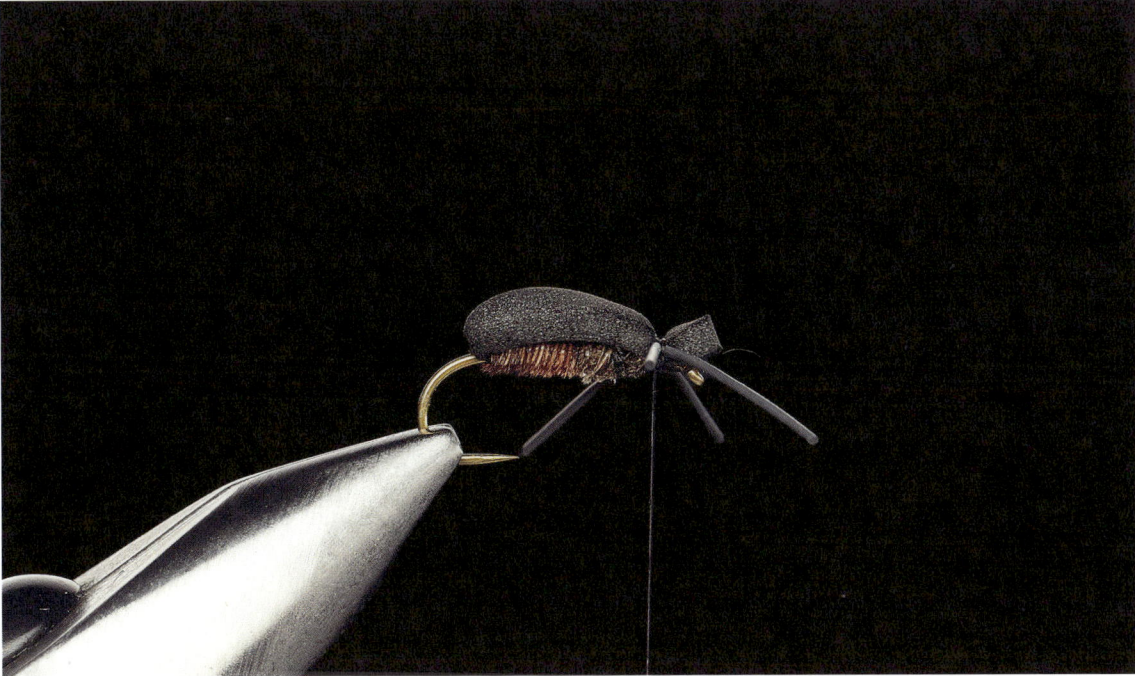

.04 While binding down the foam, tie in one strand of fine rubber on each side to form the legs. The rubber should be tied in the middle so that two legs are created on each side.

.05 In the same spot, tie in a bit of brightly colored foam for visibility and trim the butts of both.

Perfect Light

Last winter we arrived at the spring creek near Livingston, Montana, at ten o'clock on a bright forty-five-degree day. A south wind kicked up tiny waves on the quiet pools as I sat on the bank tying a 6X tippet to my twelve-foot leader, anticipating midges emerging and trout feeding on them in the next hour. A brown mink patrolled the nearby shoreline in search of a mouse, side-eyeing me as it slithered by, nosing and rummaging through the streamside grasses as it proceeded upstream. About a rod's length below the critter a fish rose, then quickly rose again. The light was perfect to see under the surface and into the quiet, six-inch-deep shallow water. It was a brown trout about fifteen inches long. No monster, but on a Montana day in early January, it sure seemed huge. I quickly knotted on a #16 Pheasant Tail Beetle that I always have secured and handy on my vest's fly patch. I presented a short, accurate cast about three feet upstream of the trout. As soon as the fly plopped down in the water, the fish raced up and took it in with an audible slurp. Excitedly, I set the hook as if this were a huge largemouth bass and promptly busted the fragile 6X tippet. Over the next hour, waiting for midges to emerge, I hooked and landed four nice rainbows on a Pheasant Tail Beetle. Lesson learned.

–C.M.

At no other time of the fishing year will the dry-fly angler find more rising fish than during winter midge activity. JEREMY KORESKI

Anadromous Fishing

with Pheasant Tails

Yvon Chouinard

"Oh, and lest I forget, it has unquestionably been my dozens of Gaspé adventures that taught me what I consider the most noteworthy salmon fishing lessons of all. First is the importance of observation and patience, second is just how much more salmon and trout fishing have in common with regards to fly choice."

– Art Lee
Atlantic Salmon Journal

In 2015, I experimented with trout fishing all year with only the Pheasant Tail Soft Hackle. I also applied the experiment to Atlantic salmon, steelhead, and various sea-run trout.

In early July on the Hawke River in Labrador I had very good luck using size 10 and 12 Pheasant Tail Soft Hackles on low-water salmon hooks, fishing them just under the surface with the greased-line method.

Later, on the Haffjarðará River in Iceland, I had similar luck. Most of the fish were grilse, with the occasional salmon. I used the sensitivity of a ten-foot, five-weight rod to give action to the fly. The occasional twitch with a hitched fly was especially effective in inducing explosive takes in the slower water.

Y.C. fishing for steelhead. Skeena River, British Columbia. STEVE PERIH

In September, I had the opportunity to fish for steelhead for five days on the Babine River in British Columbia. On the first day, visibility was only six inches. It cleared off to a foot on the second day, but I had no confidence that a fish would be able to see my small, drab pheasant tail flies. I caved in to the conditions and put on a sink tip with a big, dark Intruder, and caught one small steelhead.

On the third day, I still couldn't see my boots, but the water was somewhat clearer and the parr were active in the shallows, feeding on caddis and Green Drakes in the afternoon. I thought if the parr could see the tiny naturals, then surely the adults could see my size 10 Pheasant Tail. Sure enough, when I switched to the Pheasant Tail Soft Hackle, I started catching some large steelhead. I even caught two sockeye, which was unusual so late in the season and so far from the sea.

Conditions continued to improve, and I switched to a floating line and a hitched Pheasant Tail Soft Hackle. Even when fishing behind other anglers who were throwing gaudy traditional steelhead flies, the PT was producing fish up to thirty-seven inches. Often, when using large foam-rubber waking flies for steelhead, you get boils but no takes. I believe this is because the flies are too large. Rarely do I get a boil-and-miss with the small flies. In the clearing water of the Babine, I'm convinced the riffle-hitched, waking Pheasant Tail was the most effective fly and technique I could have used.

It's been said that anadromous fish take flies (even though they are supposedly not feeding) because they remember when they were parr and eating insects. If that's so, it would explain why

A large wild steelhead with big shoulders is released on British Columbia's Dean River. CHASE WHITE

a small fly works so well. We humans think of ourselves as perpetual teenagers; apparently, many salmon and steelhead do, too.

Another line of reasoning is that they *do* feed, even though it's rare to find anything in their stomachs. A fish biologist I met in Scotland told me that salmon clearly take natural flies after they enter fresh water. His theory is that they take in a fly, squeeze the high-protein juice out of it, then spit out the body, which is probably indigestible in their dormant stomachs. This would explain why we need to avoid the dreaded *trout set* on anadromous fish. Give them time to squeeze out that juice.

My friend Paul Bruun told me that the Reverend Dan Abrams had observed cutthroats in Yellowstone taking in grasshoppers, releasing them, taking them in again, and spitting them out up to three times before letting them go. Did they also just want that high-protein juice?

The summer of 2021 was an extreme drought year in Eastern Canada, even in northern Labrador. There was no rain from July to September. Large salmon were in the upper Flowers River, but the salmon were what the British call "dour." In these conditions, they were very reluctant to rise to our traditional bee-pattern dry flies. The usual solution to such conditions is to use small wet flies on low-water hooks. I knew what must be done.

I had a few size 14 Pheasant Tail Flymphs tied on 2X short, 2X heavy hooks. The short shanks make the flies closer to a size 16. The hitched fly waking on the surface or just below on a greased-line swing woke the salmon up. I proceeded to land fish up to almost thirty pounds. I tried a size 12 and they wouldn't touch it.

How many salmon would you catch if you were using those old traditional flies of the nineteenth century, like a fully dressed Jock Scott on a 2/0 hook? Maybe a few on the large rivers like

Connecting with a mighty steelhead on the Skeena
River, British Columbia. STEVE PERIH

the Alta, where they still kill fish. In other places where catch and release is the norm, the fish have evolved to view big flies not as something toothsome, but as something dangerous.

So, if salmon and steelhead do feed on small insects, why not fish for them as if they were just large brown trout and rainbows?

In the early days of fishing for sea trout on the Rio Grande in Argentina, we mostly swung and stripped large streamers. Later, the British came and showed us how to fish with the same small wet flies and nymphs they used on their sea trout in the United Kingdom. It changed the game.

I used to fish big streamers for pre-spawning browns in Wyoming and Montana. Now I exclusively fish the Pheasant Tail Flymphs in surprisingly small sizes and catch way more fish.

Technique

Wet Flies

Watch the video: Fishing for salmon with soft hackles

Normally, when swinging wet flies for steelhead, you mend the line upstream to slow the drift of the fly. With Atlantic salmon, you mend downstream to speed it up, as salmon prefer to take a faster fly. In both cases, you want the fly to swim across in front of the fish's head, presenting a side profile of the fly. (It's the same technique with tarpon.)

With Flymphs, I've found better success making multiple mends to avoid the swinging as much as possible. Just like with trout, the take is usually at the end of the swing when the fly is rising, looking like an emerger. A tiny twitch or strip of the line often results in an explosive take.

Fishing straight downstream, I like to leave a foot of line out of the reel, which I release when there's a take. This gives the fish time to turn and pull the hook into that sweet spot. When I'm using the tip of a light rod to give the twitch, I back off the drag to let the fish take the line. Either way works on trout or salmon.

There's nothing special about tying the Pheasant Tail Soft Hackle for salmon or steelhead. They are tied the same as for trout. Just make sure the hooks are strong enough to hold up to these bigger fish. *Note:* Be sure to test your hooks, as not all brands are equal in strength.

Dry Flies

In 2023, my go-to fly for salmon in Labrador was a size 12 Pheasant Tail X Caddis dry fly. It worked even when I got refusals on the usual bee and bug dry patterns. When I used up the three X Caddis flies I had brought with me, I tried the classic Elk Hair Caddis, but it failed to fool a single salmon—perhaps because it has a dubbed body and a palmered hackle, and thus floats high on the surface.

I don't use a tapered leader; instead, I attach ten to twelve feet of 2X tippet, which I find gives a longer dead drift to my dry fly. My friend Jim Lawley taught me a great way to hitch a fly using a down-turned eye hook: Pass the tippet through the bottom of the eye and tie a turle knot. This way the leader pulls it the same as if you had made a couple of half hitches on the shank behind the eye. This technique works for hitching soft hackles or dry flies, and you don't have to tie the hitch on one side or the other depending on which side of the river you're on.

Salmon success with Y.C. MAURO MAZZO

I use a slower-action six- to eight-weight, nine-foot rod, which is enough to handle any salmon, and the slower action protects the lighter leader.

I tie the X Caddis with the hitch knot and fish it with no drag. If I don't get a take, I let the fly continue downstream where it will start waking, thus giving two chances to hook a fish on the same cast. I've hooked several salmon that I didn't know were below me on the stream in this way.

I can't say the success I've had fishing for salmon with trout soft hackles and dry flies can be repeated in other parts of the salmon world. Salmon are incredibly complex and moody fish, with a logic that is inscrutable. Hundreds of books have been written trying to analyze their behavior, but at the end of every day we fish for them, we learn a little more, and that keeps us fishing.

To hitch a fly with a down-turned eye hook, pass the tippet through the bottom of the eye, then tie a turle knot.

149

A STORY

Sinking versus Floating Lines

One June on Russia's Rynda River, the early-season fish were flooding into the river, jumping as they entered a pool and jumping as they left. The river was high, and someone told me to use a sinking line. I did, and the result was ten takes with zero fish landed. Zero! The problem was the fly was at the same depth as the swimming salmon. They took the fly lightly and continued upstream. When I switched to a floating line, I started to land fish because the salmon rose to take the fly and then went down, thus hooking themselves in the sweet spot—the corner of the mouth.

–Y.C.

Steelhead in British Columbia. CHASE WHITE

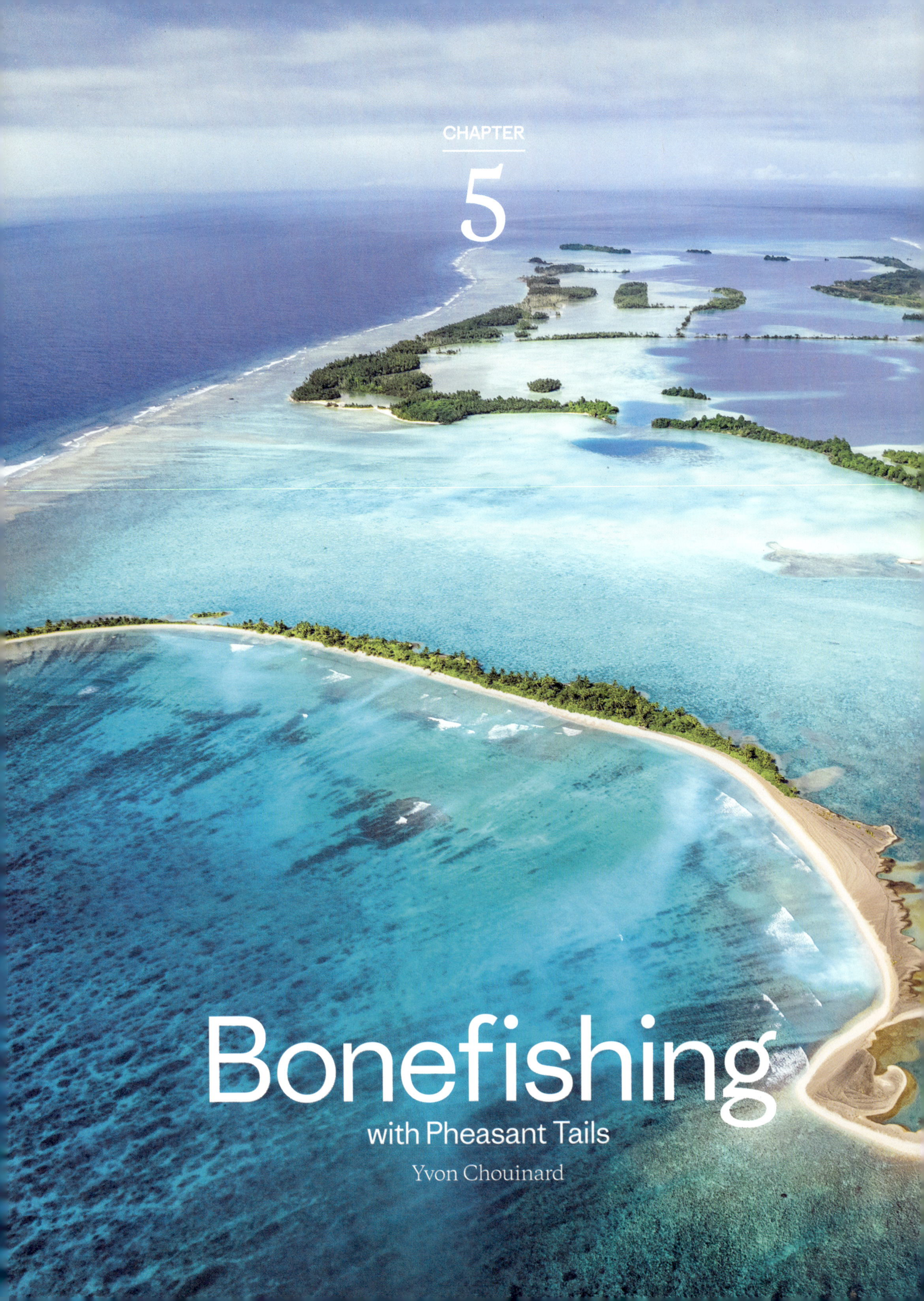

CHAPTER

5

Bonefishing

with Pheasant Tails

Yvon Chouinard

In 2001, The Nature Conservancy asked me if I wanted to go to Palmyra Atoll, south of Hawaiʻi, to catch and tag as many bonefish as possible—all in the name of science, of course. These were real country fish that had never seen a fly and had no fear of humans. They were so trusting I had a couple swim between my legs. I caught a lot of fish. Now you're no longer allowed to fish for bonefish around the island: The sharks have learned to follow the anglers and pick off every hooked fish.

Bonefish enjoy a varied diet of shrimp, crabs, worms, snails, minnows, and even spiny sea urchins. When they haven't been fished over, they will take any one of the thousands of fly patterns. They don't stray far from their local flats, except to spawn in the deep oceans. Then they come right back to their home neighborhood. There is a fourteen-pound fish in Hawaiʻi that my friends have repeatedly caught on the same flat.

When they've been fished over a lot, bonefish become extremely selective and skittish. They are onto us. They can see the guide up high on his platform way before the angler on the bow can see them. The flash of an overhead fly line and the plop of a heavy fly will send them off.

Opposite: Eastern end of Palmyra Atoll with Barren Island in the foreground. RICHARD BROOKS/ SCIENCE PHOTO LIBRARY

Above: Bahamas bonefishing. MARCOS FURER

When you swing a fly in front of their face and they "blow up," it's because they have seen enough of the silver hooks, Flashabou, and goofy eyes. Flies that used to fish well in the past no longer work, and every year new patterns are invented. They become "the fly of the year" until they, too, stop working.

Ever since 2015, when I limited myself to fishing only the Pheasant Tail Soft Hackle, I've continued to use it exclusively for all my bonefishing. Why would a trout fly made to imitate an emerging mayfly or caddis be so attractive to a bottom-feeding saltwater fish? Beats me. It's proven itself in Hawai'i, Belize, Cuba, the Seychelles, and all over the Bahamas. I'm not saying it always works. There are times of weird atmospheric pressure or slack tide when the fish just don't feel like eating anything. Other times, they'll eagerly jump on any fly that's properly presented. A Bahamian guide told me he has a client who fishes only with colored bare hooks, and he catches lots of fish. But there have been many times when the Pheasant Tail saved the day, and even when fishing's good across the board, it tends to outproduce the more traditional bonefish flies.

Of all the aspects involved in successfully fly fishing for bonefish, I would argue that number one in importance is getting the fly to the bottom. Many anglers make the mistake of not matching the weight of the fly to the depth of the water. This happens a lot when you are guided in a boat over a flat where the depth constantly changes. Over coral or an eelgrass bottom, it's better to use a properly weighted, weedless fly than a lighter fly to avoid snagging the bottom.

A good presentation puts the fly far enough ahead of the fish, so it doesn't get spooked by the plop of the fly. After that, make a long strip to catch the fish's attention. Then you can continue to tease the fish in whatever way you like, or just obey the barking orders of your guide.

Perhaps it's not the Pheasant Tail pattern itself that makes the biggest difference, but the pliable soft hackles waving in the water, and the natural shades of brown look and feel like a wide variety of bonefish food—at least, a lot more than all the synthetic fur, flashy tinsel, and painted eyes of what you find in most fly shops. In my experience, this fly just flat-out works. Show 'em something different and good, in natural fibers, match the weight to the depth, and let 'em eat.

Yvon Chouinard fishing Christmas Island. VAL ATKINSON

Pheasant Tail

Saltwater Patterns

Pheasant Tail
Bonefish

A school of gray ghosts moves between flats. IAN WILSON-NAVARRO

Pheasant Tail

Bonefish

The general rule of using a light-colored fly with a light-sand bottom, and a dark-colored fly with a dark bottom doesn't have to apply to pheasant tail flies. I've found that the PT works equally well on a light sand or dark bottom.

In shallow water, I generally use larger flies for larger fish and smaller flies for smaller fish. What's important is to have different sizes in different weights. I also use jig hooks, which give good action to the fly, and because they ride upside down, they avoid snagging the bottom. Also, I recommend having a few weedless versions in the box. Do not use stainless steel saltwater hooks (too weak) or any silver or chrome-plated hooks (too bright). The one drawback is that you need to rinse these flies thoroughly with fresh water after fishing to avoid corrosion.

MATERIALS

Hook: Umpqua U560BL-BN, #8–#12; Umpqua U555 Jig, #8–#12

Thread: 6/0 UNI-Thread, black or olive

Eyes: Dazl-Eyes, nontoxic

Ribbing: Medium copper wire

Tails: 8-10 pheasant tail barbs

Body: Pheasant tail barbs used for tails

Thorax: Hareline Hare'e Ice Dub, peacock

Hackle: Hungarian partridge, brown back feather

Watch the step-by-step video

.01   Begin by tying in the nontoxic eyes
        behind the eye of the hook. Then coat
        the eyes and hook shank with epoxy or
        head cement.

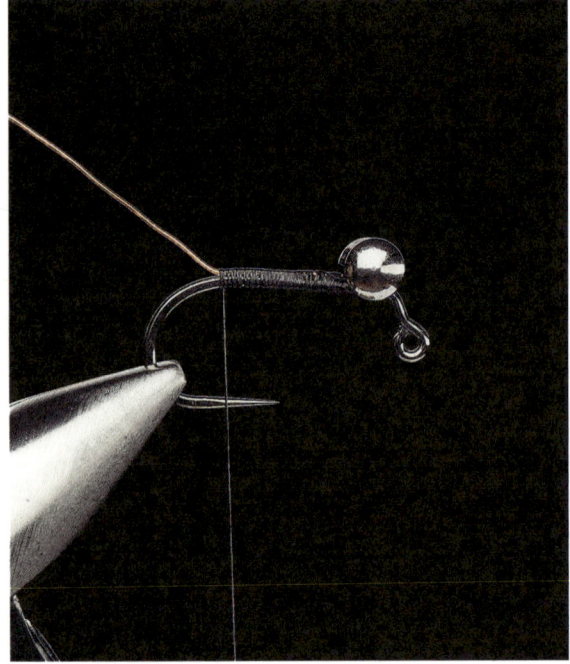

.02   Tie in the wire at the eye end of the hook;
        wrap the thread over it until you reach
        the bend.

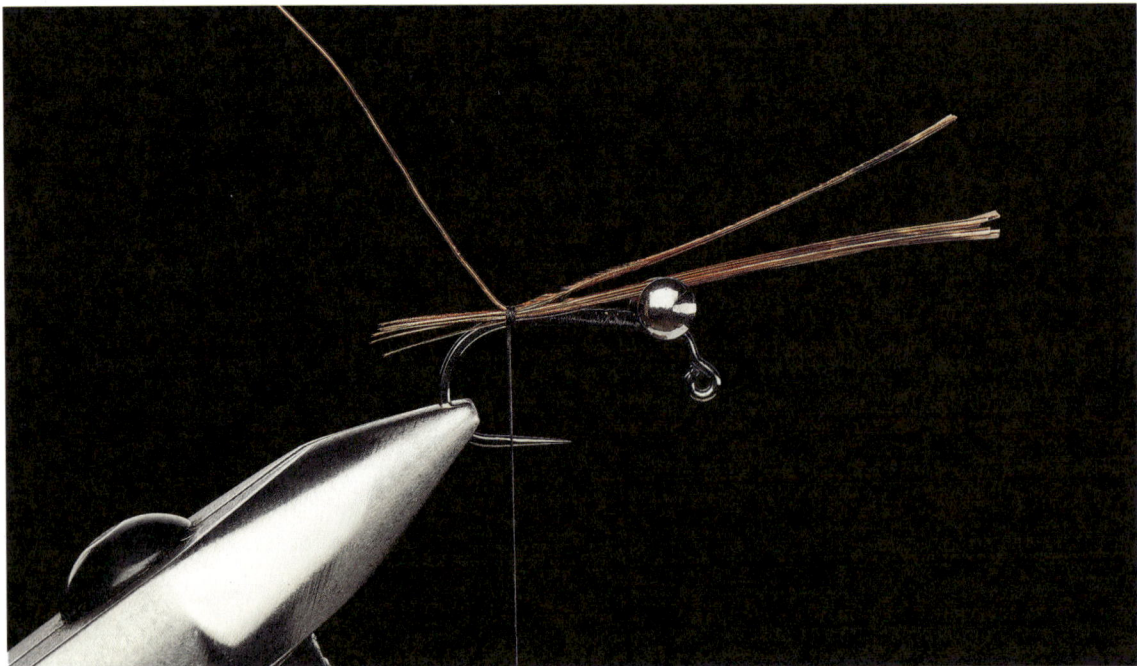

.03   Then tie in eight to ten pheasant tail barbs,
        leaving quarter-inch tails beyond the bend.

.04 Now, wrap the pheasant tail barbs forward two-thirds of the way up the hook shank to form the abdomen; tie them off and trim them.

.05 Rib the abdomen in counter-wraps with the copper wire and trim.

.06 Dub a thorax of Peacock Hare'e Ice Dub, leaving enough room to wrap the hackle behind the eyes. Wind the hackle around three times; use two hackles for hook sizes 8 to 12. Whip finish.

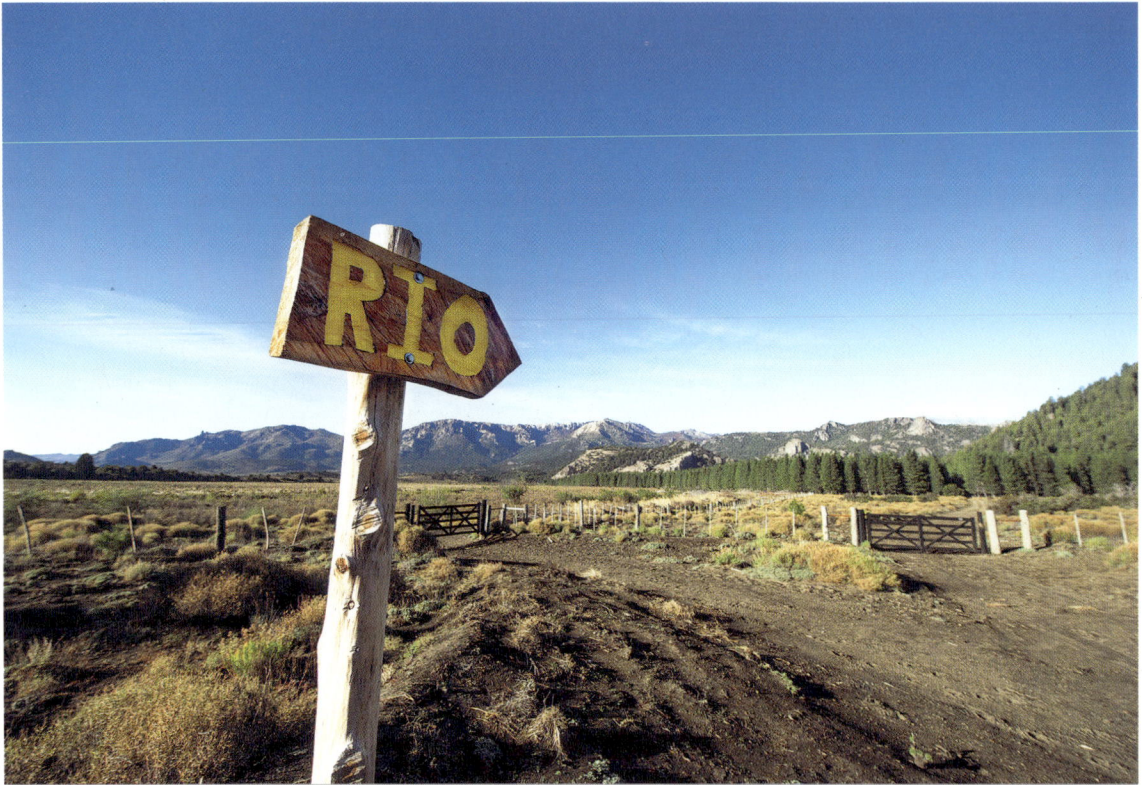

Last Cast

Pheasant tail fibers can be used in most fly designs. They are easy to obtain, inexpensive, and float well with fly floatant, so the fly requires little babysitting to keep it afloat. Without floatant, the fibers absorb water and sink well when fished wet. The fibers come in several natural colors, all from the same center tail feather, and are easier to use than dubbing for most fly tiers.

Datus Proper once remarked that we fly tiers, being complicated humans, pursue wild trout that are innocent in complex ways. Many anglers make fly tying and fishing seem like something to be conquered. However, we like to think of these pursuits as opportunities to learn. If we focus on simplicity, enjoyment, and fun, efficiency and effectiveness will follow. That's where we hope these easy Pheasant Tail fly designs come in. If we can avoid overcomplicating what is, after all, a simple endeavor, our skills and appreciation grow. To us, tying and fishing simple, effective, and easy-to-tie flies that represent what the fish recognize, key on, and are eating, while learning through the process, is what fly fishing is all about—it's not the version of fly fishing that's focused on numbers or sizes of trout.

We enjoy designing new flies to try to fool selective trout; however, we usually realize our time is much better spent sitting on the bank or on a rock closely observing the natural insects and how trout react to them. While we used to, and sometimes still do, blame the fly pattern we are using, or the size or length of the tippet, or the wind, or weather conditions for a big selective trout refusing to take the fly, we discover that most times it's not the fly on the end of our tippet that's the problem; it's our presentation that's to blame.

When you get close to the fish and observe the insects they are feeding on, and present accurate casts without relying on the latest-and-greatest fly line technology that allows you to boom out long casts, you will have the best results. By getting close, you can watch the fish as it reacts to your fly. Patient observation is the key to catching big selective trout. By learning the fundamental techniques and tying the simple fly patterns in this book, you will catch more and larger trout.

You may be thinking that we are extreme purists committed to fishing only with Pheasant Tail flies for the rest of our lives. We confess that in extremis we have resorted to tying on three-inch-long rubber club sandwiches, San Juan Worms, or God forbid, an orange or chartreuse Mop Fly.

Even with our combined two hundred years of trying to fool trout, a successful day of fishing for us is one when we learn something new and can't wait to get back to the tying desk.

Yvon Chouinard, Craig Mathews, and Mauro Mazzo

Biographies

Yvon Chouinard,

a noted fly fisher (chosen by *Fly Rod & Reel* as Angler of the Year in 2009) and environmentalist, is the founder of Patagonia, Inc. He cofounded, with Craig Mathews, 1% for the Planet, a group of businesses giving back to the environment. He lives in Ventura, California.

Craig Mathews,

with his wife, Jackie, is the founder of Blue Ribbon Flies, a retail fly-fishing store and outfitter based in West Yellowstone, Montana. Craig has authored and co-authored nine books on fly fishing in the western United States and Yellowstone National Park. He was chosen by *Fly Rod & Reel* as Angler of the Year in 2005. He and Jackie live in the Madison River Valley of Montana.

Mauro Mazzo

is an FFF Certified Master and THCI Casting Instructor, and he writes and photographs on a regular basis for European fly-fishing magazines. He has fished around the globe from the Italian Alps to Himachal Pradesh, from Cuba to the Kola Peninsula. He lives in Milan, Italy.

Index

Next spread: Angler Y.C. on a Patagonia river.
BRYAN GREGSON

167